Praise for Holli Kenley's *SHIFTING Bravely*

Once again, Holli Kenley takes the mystery out of what can be accomplished when people find the courage to change one of the most powerful of relationships—the one we have with ourselves.

Kenley weaves words together into captivating visuals of how people can be scarred and even petrified—yet keep turning the keys that open the doors into the compelling insights that chase away fear and confusion.

SHIFTING Bravely is a beautifully written, easy to digest invitation and guide for personal growth, filled with illustrations of how those who gave themselves permission to heal deeply buried wounds were able to step into their real story and create powerfully grounded energy for profound, untethered life-long change.

Debra Rock, MSW, LCSW, psychotherapist in private practice

Wrapped in the metaphor of the changing seasons, *SHIFTING Bravely* will take you on a powerful journey of growth, healing and transformation. Part guidebook, part almanac, *SHIFTING Bravely* brilliantly describes the phases of personal metamorphosis and offers profound insight, concrete information and practical tools and exercises to skillfully and lovingly navigate the journey into oneself.

Marcie R. Elias, JD, MA, organizational psychologist

We are all called to SHIFT at some point in our lives, but often, the fear of what that could entail paralyzes us. In Holli Kenley's beautiful book, *SHIFTING Bravely*, she lovingly guides you towards your SHIFT so that you can step courageously into it and create lasting change. Filled with real-life stories, practical tools and reflections, Kenley's words seemed to sing right off the page and land directly into my heart. Beautifully weaved tapestry of wisdom and inspiration! A must-read for anyone who is desiring personal freedom.

Shari Alyse 'Joy Magnet', bestselling author and motivational speaker

A deep reflection of the unhealed elements in our lives, *SHIFTING Bravely* is a journey of growth that invites the reader to be vulnerable, open, and courageous. Kenley creates a safe space on the page and a feeling of connectedness with the reader. It is interactive and encourages the reader to trust the process, rest, and renew.

Allison Sucamele, PsyD, adjunct professor, Department of Education and Psychology, Course Lead Positive Psychology, Pepperdine University

SHIFTING Bravely is quite literally a life-changing book. Kenley masterfully weaves together real-life stories with easy-to-understand ways to implement changes that will help to create the life you want. If you're looking to shift your world, start with *SHIFTING Bravely*.

Kiersten Hathcock, author *Little Voices*, CEO Mod Mom Furniture

By following the Flower's seasonal journey of self-growth in *Shifting Bravely*, we get inspired and encouraged to carefully and purposefully tend to our own seeds. With the help of exercises throughout different seasons, we are able to grow (our seeds) towards significant sustainable change. This is a great book!

Ilse Aerts, LMFT, LPCC

Rich in mood and atmosphere, *SHIFTING Bravely* takes us through the journeys of multiple transformative experiences and healing modalities while illuminating a peaceful approach full of possibility for change. So thoughtfully told, anyone can glean tools for their own transformation.

Charlotte Carson, Founder CLEARlife

By sharing the how's and why's some individuals chose to shift their lives, emotions, and beliefs, Kenley draws us in to experience the realities and reasons for transforming our own. The exercises at the end of each chapter bring readers forward on their journeys. Great reading! I pray *SHIFTING Bravely* gets out to many readers!

Barbara Sinor, Ph.D.,
author of *Inspirational Musings: Insights Through Healing*

This entire book is a beautiful metaphor, captured by the picture on the cover. Holli guides the reader along the path of growth from unacknowledged damage through gradual awakening due to suffering, to metamorphosis into strength. She explores what can stand in the way of progress, and how to grow anyway. Thought- and emotion-provoking exercises at the end of each chapter enable the reader to do the necessary work: we succeed by doing, not by knowing. If life is not how you want it, allow this wise lady to guide you to a better place.

Bob Rich, Ph.D.,
author of *From Depression to Contentment: A Self-Therapy Guide*

SHIFTING Bravely
A path to Growth, Healing, and Transformation

Holli Kenley

Loving Healing Press

Ann Arbor, MI

Learn more at www.HolliKenley.com

ISBN 978-1-61599-628-5 paperback
ISBN 978-1-61599-629-2 hardcover
ISBN 978-1-61599-630-8 eBook

Distributed by Ingram (USA/CAN/AU), Bertram's Books (UK/EU)

Published by
Loving Healing Press   Tollfree 888-761-6268
5145 Pontiac Trail   FAX 734-663-6861
Ann Arbor, MI 48105

www.LHPress.com   info@LHPress.com

Audiobook editions available at Audible.com and iTunes

To The Flower

Rooted in courage and commitment,
a shift emerged out of shame.
A rising up of who you are,
inspiring others to do the same.

A SHIFT is defined as the following:

an unexpected or unpredictable compelling
transformation in your beliefs, perceptions, or
truths about you, someone else, or something

Contents

SHIFTING, My Story

Much of who I am is the result of *SHIFTING*. I have experienced it over and over again. Although I have become accustomed to embracing change, recently I became intrigued by its process. Upon returning to Southern California in 2018, I reopened my private practice as a Licensed Marriage and Family Therapist. It was after several months of working with clients again and observing their journeys of inner personal change when I came to appreciate the profound nature of *SHIFTING* and its potential for lasting impact.

When I think back over the most significant SHIFTS in my life, some emerged out of varying levels of discomfort, disappointment, or dissatisfaction. One of those SHIFTS took place during my first career as a teacher. Although I loved teaching, after twenty years I began to feel somewhat dissatisfied. I realized my passions had changed and my calling was elsewhere. I enjoyed helping others, especially adult females, lead more whole and well lives.

During my early forties, I devised, organized, and led groups for females supporting them with wellness challenges. After three years of leading the groups, I could feel my SHIFT awakening. I was being called to bring healing to others but on a more professional level. I paid attention to the calling. While I continued teaching, I entered graduate school to obtain a Masters in Psychology with an emphasis in Marriage, Family and Child Counseling. Over a period of seven years, I graduated with my degree, completed the required three thousand hours of internship, and passed both my written and oral state boards for becoming a California Licensed Marriage and Family Therapist.

This SHIFT's genesis came from a seed of dissatisfaction with one career path but was germinated within a deep passion for another. Still, its emergence was lengthy and required tremendous sacrifice and commitment. During this period of time, I was married and raising a family. I also moved from teaching middle school to taking on a demanding position at a local high school. There were times when I felt like giving up. I didn't want to write another research paper, take another exam, or as an English teacher, correct another essay. Over the seven years, resistance showed up in all kinds of shapes and forms. And yet, I learned how to anticipate it, prepare for it, and move through it. In *SHIFTING Bravely*, I share with you how to work through resistance, from both internal and external forces. Learning how to navigate resistance successfully is critical to strengthening and sustaining your emerging SHIFT.

Throughout my adult life, there have been additional SHIFTS that arose from varying levels of discomfort and dissatisfaction. Some of them included changing places of employment, or moving from unhealthy environments, or detaching from toxic relationships. All contributed to my growth and emergence in positive ways.

However, there have been numerous SHIFTS in my life birthed from deep pain buried beneath layers of shame. In my work as an author in the field of psychology, I have chronicled these SHIFTS in several of my books. The first publication was *Breaking Through Betrayal: And Recovering the Peace Within* (2009, 2016 2nd Edition).

After years of feeling betrayed by a family member and trying everything I knew how to do at the time to create a healthier relationship, I decided I needed to heal myself first. Because I wasn't satisfied with the tools available for recovery from betrayal, I began entertaining the idea of exploring betrayal and developing a treatment program specifically designed for healing from betrayal injury. As my SHIFT awakened, I realized this would require a great deal of time and effort. I thought about letting go of the idea, but the calling wouldn't subside. I paid attention to it.

Thus, I spent months studying past and present client cases, reading books on betrayal, and exploring other thinking. As I gained more insight and understanding into betrayal, I felt my SHIFT taking root. I began writing down my thoughts. As I wrote, I started implementing the strategies and practices I was creating into my life and trying out their efficacy with clients. A year went by. I continued to fine tune my strategies and to write them down. As I did so, I could feel my SHIFT emerging and strengthening. With more time, this SHIFT was sustained. I was no longer held hostage by my betrayer or the betrayals. I was free. Experiencing a growing SHIFT is one thing. Knowing how to integrate your SHIFT solidly into your being and how to sustain its presence is critical. I share these strategies with you in *SHIFTING Bravely* and provide paths for their implementation.

In my writings, I have been very transparent about trauma in my life and my recovering journeys. In 2011, *Mountain Air: Relapsing and Finding the Way Back, One Breath at a Time* was published. With twenty years of recovering under my belt, I felt I understood the nature of relapse. However, when I experienced a relapse into extremely unhealthy codependent behaviors 2008-2010, I became intimately acquainted with its relentless shame-filled presence. With the help of a skilled therapist, I embraced my recovering from relapse. More importantly, during the process I unearthed a deeply embedded trauma from childhood that served as an underlying trigger to my relapse.

From this experience, two SHIFTS emerged. One was the development of a compassionate awareness into the relationship between relapse and shame. This SHIFT in perspective altered my approach in addressing relapse with my clients and enabled me to be a more empathic therapist. The other SHIFT was a growing understanding of how and why a SHIFT takes hold and solidifies itself in some individuals and how and why it doesn't for others. In other words, in Chapter Four, A SHIFT Takes Root, I explore the importance of doing the hard work of digging deep and clearing out past injuries and injustices, no matter how small or significant. I know from my own journey and that of others, if we do not do this work, our growth will be stunted or sabotaged. More importantly, I present a three-part process for tending to this delicate and difficult phase of *SHIFTING Bravely*.

Lastly, several years ago numerous SHIFTS emerged out of unspeakable traumatic events within my family. These SHIFTS transformed my life on every level and are detailed in my book *Daughters Betrayed By Their Mothers: Moving from Brokenness to Wholeness* (2018). One SHIFT, allowing myself to be vulnerable, developed years previously but it was strengthened during this painful period of growth.

In order for me to continue emerging and becoming who I am called to be, I have learned I must stand in my truths. If I choose to share them, I must do so openly and honestly. Is there risk in being vulnerable? Yes, there is great risk. Does it call for courage? Yes, vulnerability calls for immeasurable courage. However, I have come to understand that when I am the most vulnerable, I open myself up for the most growth. As you embrace your journey, you will be encouraged to do the same.

In closing, at times I have traveled my path of emergence alone and trusted my intuition. However, for most of my life, I have leaned into support systems and learned from mentors who have gone before me. I wrote *SHIFTING Bravely* so that you would not be alone. More importantly, I wanted to create a path to guide you and light your way. I have gone before you. And, I am one of you.

> "Healers aren't holy beings sent down from the light. They emerge from the darkness after learning how to heal [themselves] and radiate the glow of transformation."
>
> Unknown

Seasonal Opening

"When you assess your own life, consider it with the eye of a gardener. Underneath the surface lies rich, fertile soil waiting to nurture the seeds you sow. Even more than you can imagine will grow there if given a chance."

Steve Goodier

As the sun moves across the half-moon window positioned slightly below the ceiling on the west wall of my office, its rays cast a warm glow into the room. On an early Saturday morning, I am nestled into my therapist chair, mindful of the heavy responsibility I have been entrusted with. Time and time again, I am humbled by the depth of vulnerability before me, and I am reminded of the delicate guidance required to explore change, while unearthing its restraints. The sun continues to move west, making its morning brush against the stately clock located on the north wall. The brightness alerts me; it is time.

Welcoming in my next client, I am reminded of how I have come to think of her. She is like a Flower, whose layered essence fills the room with strength, courage, and compassion. Her beauty emanates from within, deeply ingrained in her new way of being. As the Flower flows into the room, my mind recalls the significance of her presence.

The beautiful full silky blossom positioned across from me should not have been here. Poised in the large soft-brown leathered high-back chair, she settles into the safety of our ongoing conversation. Decades of trauma have left their scars, invisible to the naked eye but unveiled over time in stories shaded with darkness. A blanket of mutual trust wraps itself around our connection providing a protected space for peeling away layers of injury buried deep within. The strong stem sustaining the Flower allows me to move further into exploring her pain. She unearths her past, hungry for truth.

After our session, I reflect upon the fragility of life and on its fleeting nature. It's remarkably easy not to pay attention to one's suffering, discomfort, or nudging. And yet, time and time again, individuals do so. Over two years ago, the injured Flower bravely entered my office and embarked upon a weekly journey of discovery, awakened to the uneasiness within. A seed, which lay dormant for years, began to move, ever so slightly and slowly.

I ask myself, "What caused her to pay attention this time? How did she know not to ignore it? Was she afraid, anxious, confused, or excited? Did she understand within that moment of silent movement she would be called upon to be vulnerable, courageous and committed, more than ever before?"

Pondering those questions, I continue to reflect on the ensuing mysteries of change. How is it that sometimes growth continues and is sustainable while at other times, it is not? Is it because the soil must be carefully tended to so it will welcome new seeds, making room for additional growth? Or is new growth often stunted by resistance, from both internal and external forces? What other factors come into play?

In order to broaden my lens, I have invited individuals to submit their stories of "A SHIFT In My Life" [Appendix A]. I will draw upon their stories of shifting, as well as the experiences of numerous clients whose journeys led them through a seasonal process of self-growth. Names of participants and clients have been changed.

I want to know more about this process—SHIFTING Bravely. I want to answer the questions I posed above and address additional mysteries. I want to be able to offer insights and lessons into this dynamic process for individuals who are currently working through dissatisfying circumstances, discomfort, or dis-ease in their lives. I want to offer a pathway of transformation to any individual yearning for significant and sustainable change.

Inspired by the messages within Steve Goodier's quote, "When you assess your own life, consider it with the eye of a gardener," I have defined a process of SHIFTING Bravely. Through the lens of a gardener, you will not only learn how to assess your life, but you will learn how to decipher, unearth, and nurture seeds of change which lie within you.

To guide your path, SHIFTING Bravely has been organized around a seasonal process of growth. The four earthly seasons—Winter, Spring, Summer, and Autumn—are symbolic of the four seasons of growth within our shifting process. As you move through Winter Stillness, Spring Stirrings, Summer Strong, and Autumn Splendor, a path to growth, healing and transformation will mirror that of a garden—from its genesis to its harvest.

Within each season, the delicate and demanding process of *SHIFTING Bravely* is broken down into chapters—each unraveling the mysteries of change while specifically providing strategies integral to implementing the growing process. And, in order to engage and support readers in their journeys of *SHIFTING Bravely*, each chapter will conclude with follow-up exercises.

This is important. If it is your desire to travel this path, it is beneficial to acclimate yourself to the content and to the shifting process by reading through the entire book, at a comfortable pace. Then, you are strongly encouraged to go back, re-read each chapter, allowing the information to soak in more fully. Grab hold of a journal or notebook and spend as much time as needed completing the exercises for each chapter before moving onto the next chapter. It is going to require hard work, commitment, and courage. And, it is going to require you to trust this truth—"...[Your]...soil is waiting to nurture the seeds you sow. Even more than you can imagine will grow there if given a chance." (Goodier)

My mind returns to the tender but tenacious blossom and her journey. Throughout the winter, spring, summer, and fall seasons, I have been sensitive to her needs for rest and renewal, and carefully waited for her surges of resilience. However, I have found it is during those moments of stillness and of carefully crafted questioning when another seed is unearthed...and something shifts. I can feel it. The Flower can too. We see it in each other's eyes. It is remarkable.

The process of *SHIFTING Bravely* is extraordinary. Let's explore and experience it together.

Season One: Winter Stillness

1 A SHIFT Lies Dormant

"Every person has seeds of greatness within, even
though they may currently be dormant."

John C. Maxwell

Shifting is a process of growth. Its genesis—seeds. Remarkably, we carry
them within us. How is it we do not know of their existence? What is it
we are doing or not doing that contributes to their dormancy? What is
behind this mystery?

As we explore why our seeds "may currently be dormant," we begin
by understanding there is no deficiency within the seeds themselves. Nor
is it a fault of our own, or not noticing them, or not searching hard
enough. The awareness to do so is simply not available to us. It is
important to embrace this truth.

We are shielded from dormant seeds by various forms of camouflage—disruptions and diversions which consume us and often control
the course of our lives.

Forms of camouflage are deceptive. Their presence often appears to
provide us with opportunities for growth or change, at least in self-
satisfying or superficial ways. On closer examination, forms of
camouflage typically limit our growth, conforming us to patterns of
survival, some beneficial and some not. In order to begin the process of
acknowledging sleepy seeds and of discerning their presence, we must
familiarize ourselves with the most prevalent forms of camouflage. Only
then can we understand the concept of *SHIFTING Bravely* and begin our
journey through a seasonal process of self-growth.

One common form of camouflage is stagnation and settling. Many of
us have come to accept that getting by is good enough, even if we feel
stuck or unsatisfied. Others of us, who know we are not living up to our
potential or pursuing our dreams, feel trapped and resigned to

predetermined destinies. Day after day, our growth is stunted by settling for a degree of security and stagnating in mundane routines. How does this happen?

Because diverse internal and external sources of influence shape our developmental years as well as our own choices, we enter into young adult years with perceptions and expectations regarding self-efficacy. Some of us view ourselves as independent, free to choose what we want for ourselves and our lives. Others of us may feel obligated, or in many cases, bound or oppressed by our circumstances, forcing us to settle for something we do not want.

Stagnation and settling shroud our thinking with self-doubt and self-blame. More importantly, over time and with repetition of behavioral patterns, these agents of camouflage condition us into believing we don't deserve anything more, anything better, or different. Or perhaps on some level, we convince ourselves we should be grateful for what we have and what we know.

From the many stories I received regarding "A SHIFT in My Life," let's begin with Robert's experience. His words convey the dormant nature of his seeds, settling for what he was taught and feeling resigned with the status quo—securing a future for himself.

> In 1951, my folks bought an old estate near Denver. I was twelve years old. From that time, until I was twenty-eight, my family focused on building and operating a small family country club on that property. Everyone involved assumed I would eventually take over the business. I was involved in every aspect of building, maintenance, working with the public, lifeguarding, promoting, and in fact every facet of the business and its future development.
>
> Finishing high school in 1957, I was urged to go on to college and get a teaching certificate. In 1961, I added teaching high school to my life. I found teaching to be a real challenge and joy but was committed to building the club and becoming economically independent. The school schedule complimented my summer obligations. In the early 60s, I began designing and promoting a year-round club.
>
> I was also involved with forming several marketing enterprises. I worked 24/7 365 days a year. Fully engaged in that life, I was sure my future was secure.

Robert accomplished what was expected of him. His loyalty to his family and to the business rewarded him financially. Although settling and stagnation served him well for a period of time, the seeds of a more fulfilling dream lay dormant under layers of monetary success. In Robert's words, "I added teaching high school to my life. I found teaching to be a real challenge and joy but was committed to building the club and becoming economically independent."

Another form of camouflage that presents itself in countless individuals is psychological pain. Some of the most common disorders such as anxiety, depression, Posttraumatic Stress Disorder (PTSD), and behavioral / substance addiction wreak havoc with our lives. Their causes are complex and complicated. Their symptoms can be chronic and debilitating. When they are unattended or when denial prevents their acknowledgement, we are held hostage to their manifestations. And thus, disturbance determines our destiny, shutting out other pathways to growth.

When disorders are diagnosed and addressed, effective psychological interventions as well as medical treatments require compliance and commitment, focusing our energies and resources on symptom reduction and management. This is as it should be. Our mental health must remain a priority. Therefore, it is understandable why dormant seeds of change remain in their states of hibernation, as individuals courageously explore their roots of pain and embrace their recovering journeys.

From her story, "A SHIFT In My Life," Annika's words speak to this form of camouflage.

> Back in December of 2010, I somehow was brought to my knees and surrendered to my alcoholism. I went into treatment in Eugene, Oregon, for only twenty-one days. At the time I went into treatment, I was forty-four years old. I had managed to destroy my marriage, relationships, trust, and all of my self-worth and dignity.
>
> When I got out of treatment, I had nothing to go home to. No house, no car, and even my kids didn't like me. I lived in Oregon and was actually shunned by my community due to my behavior while I was drinking...it was bad. I don't blame anyone.
>
> I ended up getting a job in [the field of] sobriety. They call that first recovery job "a get-well job." I worked as many hours as possible while attending intensive outpatient treatment.

As Annika's story illustrates, her addiction to alcohol impacted her psychological and relational health. Making her recovery a priority, she focused her energies on a twenty-one-day treatment program. Thus, during periods of camouflage requiring rigorous focus and concentrated investment into recovery, the cultivation of an awareness of seeds within dormant states can be stymied, or as in Annika's case, it can be redirected towards self-care.

Often psychological disturbance is accompanied with physiological disease. Or vice-versa. Either way, disease of any kind, especially if it is chronic in nature, requires tremendous investment into our healing. And thus, just as with psychological disturbance, there may be periods of time in our lives where our physical health dictates our path and our priorities. This type of camouflage takes on a protective role of sorts, unintentionally helping us by redirecting our attention away from dormant seeds. Our bodies and minds are in weakened states, calling on us to pay attention to them.

Dedicated educator Britt describes in her story, "A SHIFT In My Life," how illness caught her off guard, redirecting her energies from her beloved work as she began searching for causes and exploring treatments. Remarkably, as Britt tended to her physiological disease, she began to unearth dormant seeds nestled beneath her layers of camouflage.

> As I moved through my twenties and thirties many good things came my way. I was happily married to my life partner and together we built one of the pre-eminent archaeological education and research centers in the nation. My husband and I worked hard, dreamed large, and were wildly successful. For all its rewards, the work was exhausting and not without a constant stream of crises and stress.
>
> After our two sons were born, we retired from our position of leadership at the education center we had created. It seemed creating schools was in our blood. By the time our sons were four and six, we moved to Arizona to take care of my husband's parents. We soon became involved in the charter school movement and successfully created the second charter school in the state—an exportable model on the forefront of education. I was in my mid-forties by this time, raising two sons, working...trying to juggle it all.
>
> Around this time, much to my amazement, I discovered I had developed significant gut issues which required treatment—potentially Crohn's disease they said. It can be a nasty one. I was taken by surprise. I had always been physically strong and rarely sick with anything. I began to focus on the reasons why my gut

was crying out to get my attention. I ended up following a comprehensive three-pronged approach.

As Britt's story portrays, it is important to note that psychological disorders or physiological diseases can be the impetus for uncovering layers of camouflage as individuals begin to question the challenges they face and search for trusted direction and tested remedies. However, it has been my experience with most individuals who are in the midst of life-threatening storms, it is critical to channel their energies on their healing practices and treatment plans required of them. Once the turbulent nature of the storm has passed and when a layer or two of camouflage has been slowly cleared away, we become more settled. In that stillness, dormant seeds lie, waiting.

Additionally and importantly, one of the most formidable forms of camouflage which tethers us to a place of unknowing, and thus a lack of awareness for change, shows up within our maladaptive thought processes, or what I refer to as self-shaming life messages.

Life messages are an individual's internal dialogue (or messaging) composed from each person's unique life experiences and perceptions of them. Although life messages could come from any external source of influence, we are predominately impacted by those coming from our primary caregivers. Life messages are powerful. They form our personal truths about ourselves and our inner personal value.

In the twenty-five years I have worked with victims of abuse, betrayal, and trauma of all kinds, I have found destructive life messages of self-blame, self-shame, and self-devaluation are largely responsible for individuals' negative self-image as well as their lack of self-worth and self-efficacy. Because these distorted life messages typically have been deeply engrained since childhood, their dominant nature easily camouflages seeds of change, shrouding their dormancy and smothering possibilities of alternative ways of being.

In one of the stories submitted for "A SHIFT In My Life," Margot shared her experience growing up in a highly troubled, dysfunctional family. In her story, she references her disturbed step-mother who had Borderline Personality Disorder (BPD). Before we turn to Margot's story, it is important to touch upon the nature and complexity of BPD.

According to the *Diagnostic and Statistical Manual for Mental Disorders: Fifth Edition*, (DSM-5), Borderline Personality Disorder is defined as a "pervasive pattern of instability of interpersonal relation-ships, self-image, affects [feelings, emotions, moods], and marked impulsivity" (DSM-5, p.663). These patterns of instability begin to show up in early adulthood. While healthy individuals are able to negotiate tension, accommodate differences, or accept challenges in relationships, individuals with BPD respond quite differently. They will demonstrate "inappropriate anger, sudden despair, erratic mood swings, and panic or fury in response to challenges or any tension or distress" (DSM-5, p.663).

These reactive, unstable, and impulsive behaviors are an attempt to "make frantic efforts to avoid real or imagined abandonment" (DSM-5, p.663). In other words, fearing they are being rejected or abandoned, they will turn on others suddenly or reject them first to avoid such feelings. Although there are other destructive behaviors characteristic of BPD, clients I have worked with often describe their relationships with a Borderline as abusive, chaotic, and exhausting. For children raised by a Borderline parent, it can be frightening and isolating growing up, as they are unable to tether themselves to a source of safety, security, and unconditional love in their own home. In addition, the severely unpredictable nature of living in a home with a BPD parent or a substance/alcohol abusing household can lead to cognitive disturbance and emotional stress among children who are conditioned to anticipate when and where danger will strike. Needless to say, the needs of children are lost in environments of confusion and chaos characteristic of BPD.

The impact of Borderline Personality Disorder as well as other destructive family dynamics are quite evident in Margot's story. A few of her life messages vividly illustrate their painful presence.

> I was the "accident" that happened when my sisters were six and ten. I heard I was a colicky and difficult baby for my mother, who was chronically clinically depressed, and somewhat aloof and caustic. She taught me to tiptoe around our father so as not to upset him. Looking back, I see that my mother was emotionally abused by him, as were we three girls.
>
> I have no real loving memories of my mother. Later in life a psychic told me that all she had to give me was my birth. My dad could be fun, but he had a temper and mental illness. He drank too much, which turned him into a raging tyrant. At other times, he was like a child, naked and prancing from the bathroom to the bedroom from a shower, giggling all the way.
>
> My mother died when I was nine and after the funeral, no one talked about it. My father remarried when I was ten to an alcoholic woman who had both Borderline Personality Disorder and Obsessive-Compulsive Disorder. She was nice in public but at home they got into violent fights and she would harangue me

after school while I was trying to do my homework. I was a good kid, got into no trouble, and got good grades but I could never do anything right. She would go on and on when drunk, comparing my sisters and me to her three boys. We could never measure up. Between my dad and my stepmother, I was miserable and suicidal, although I could not bring myself to take my own life.

Our life messages not only impact how we view ourselves but also how we feel about ourselves. In Margot's story, her life messages of being an accident—"all my mother had to give me was my birth"—and of being a failure—"I could never do anything right"—fueled her sense of worthlessness and suicidal thoughts. As shame-filled life messages such as Margot's are reinforced through chronic neglectful, abusive behaviors and without opportunities to have destructive messages countered or negated, they become deeply embedded self-truths. These toxic layers of camouflage are sown within the soil, suffocating seeds of change and exiling them to their states of dormancy.

There are additional forms of camouflage. However, other than the more common forms we have already unearthed, I have found camouflage is all around us. It is in anyone and anything pulling our attention outward. This could be a partner or child, healthy or unhealthy. This may be a profession or a passion that consumes our time and energy.

It is *any* source of external influence or interest in which we choose to invest ourselves. And it is when we begin to over-invest into someone or something—where our worth is determined predominantly by our degree of investment—that we unwittingly place ourselves in a posture of unknowing.

Enrique's story from "A SHIFT In My Life" portrays this form of camouflage.

> For the past twenty-five years, I had been teaching psychology part time and conducting my private practice as a Marriage and Family Therapist mostly full time. In December 2019, I retired from teaching. I had absolutely no idea that the teaching was taking so much time and energy. I had been developing a few physical problems over the years and just went from doctor to specialist to doctor. Over the years, family and friends told me to take it easy and not work so hard.
>
> I explained that I came from a family of workers and quoted my mother: "I would rather wear out than rust out." I grew up

on a farm and the work never ended. Somehow, I thought that is the way life was. Besides, I loved teaching and psychotherapy.

As Enrique's story depicts, by attaching ourselves to external sources of worth such as relationships, careers, possessions or social pastimes, our developing awareness into internal sources of value and meaningful growth is overshadowed by the importance of other people, places, and things and our degree of investment into them. Navigating from an external locus of control, we remain shielded from the possibilities of change forming within and from their genesis—seeds.

Drawing from the stories of "A SHIFT In My Life," we have come to understand how during Winter Stillness seeds of change lie dormant when we are experiencing personal turmoil, periods of testing, and when we are pursuing investments that turn our attentions outward. We have learned that when left to run their course, these disruptions and diversions control the direction of our lives, or at the very least, contain us within our current states of being. We also have learned that by tending to our health, relationships, and personal wounds, little by little we are capable of clearing away layers of camouflage and redirecting our course. Either way, our seeds of change remain undisturbed in Winter's Stillness. The duration of their dormancy is determined by us.

The untethered Flower who found her way into my office two years ago, spent over fifty years blowing in the wind. She was tossed here and there, a fragile young blossom among cruel, harsh environments. As she matured, her modes of survival taught her to give tirelessly and relentlessly to others—to please, to provide, and to produce. No time was given for pause, for reflection, only turning outward to anticipate others' needs.

Although her professional field provided her with success and security, her psychological wellbeing was constantly in a state of chaos, confusion, and overwhelm. Past unhealed trauma reared its ugly face in nightmares and flashbacks, preventing sleep and exacerbating pre-existing fragile conditions. Depression and anxiety rushed rampantly through her like untamed animals. In the insanity of it all, her seeds lay dormant, waiting for an awakening.

Exercises—A SHIFT Lies Dormant

As we enter into the early phase of Winter Stillness, we have come to understand "Every person has seeds of greatness within, even though they may currently be dormant." We learned how we are shielded from our dormant seeds by various forms of camouflage. In order to become more aware of our seeds of greatness, we must take an honest inventory of any and all people, places, and things disrupting or diverting our lives.

We also learned how forms of camouflage are deceptive. Thus, as you begin to identify yours, remember they can appear to provide you with opportunities for growth or change, at least in self-satisfying or superficial ways. However, on closer examination, forms of camouflage limit our growth.

Take as much time as you need as you conduct this exercise. Uncomfortable feelings may surface as you discover why your seeds lie dormant. It is up to you to do the work. Pause. Take a break. And then, keep going.

If you are ready, I welcome you onto your path, *SHIFTING Bravely.*

1. Reviewing and reflecting upon the different forms of camouflage, identify one (or more) that applies to you. Then, give an example of each. Most importantly, describe in detail how each is defining you and how it is playing a role in determining your course in life.

    ### Forms of Camouflage

    a. Stagnation and settling
        ➢ Examples: Living by someone else's expectations; bound or oppressed by societal or cultural norms; stuck in circumstances beyond your control; feeling this is all you deserve

    b. Psychological disturbance
        ➢ Examples: Mood disorders such as Major Depressive Disorder and anxiety disorders such as Posttraumatic Stress Disorder and Panic Disorder; Substance and behavioral addictions; other forms of trauma and abuse. Note: This is not a full list of psychological disturbances that can act as forms of camouflage in your lives.

    c. Relational dysfunction

> ➢ Examples: Family of origin dysfunction; partner relational issues, parent / child relational issues; unhealthy friendships or work relationships

d. Physiological disorders or disease
> ➢ Examples: Life-threatening diseases; physical trauma or injury; disabilities

e. Destructive life messages
> ➢ Examples: *I don't matter; I am not enough; I'm to blame; I shouldn't be here*

f. Investing primarily into external sources of worth
> ➢ Examples: Relationships; professions; pastimes; interests; hobbies

2. After identifying and naming your form/s of camouflage and explaining how they have influenced and impacted the direction of your life, answer the following questions. These are very important.

❖ What you are learning about yourself?

❖ What have you become more aware of?

❖ What surprised you?

❖ What intuitions were confirmed?

3. In A SHIFT Lies Dormant, whose story connected with you the most? Why?

2   A SHIFT Is Awakened

> "You are in a state of discomfort because old ways of being no longer serve a purpose in your life. A new version of you is being called..."
>
> Ash Alves

Winter Stillness provides a safe refuge for our seeds of change. While they lie dormant, we are tending to external calls placed upon us and to those we choose. Whether the calls are of our choosing or demanded of us, our investments into them determine our paths, some healthy and some unhealthy. Human behavior tells us that as long as we are in a state of comfort or a semblance of it, we are less likely to change what we are doing. Thus, as long as there is no need for seeds of change, they lie in wait for their call, for a reason to awaken.

The calling, signaling us that our current ways of being are no longer serving our wellbeing, emanates from a single source. That source is discomfort. None of us is a stranger to this unsettling emotion. But why is it some of us will stay in our places of discomfort while others of us will begin to move out of them? Let's explore the conditions preserving our seeds in their dormancy and those triggering sleepy seeds to open their eyes—when A SHIFT Is Awakened.

Most of us deal with varying levels of unease every day. Many of us embrace healing strategies or engage in healthy behaviors to mitigate uncomfortable feelings or situations. On the contrary, others of us turn to extreme measures to assuage or arrest intolerable levels of discomfort. In other words, we do everything in our power to manage our discomfort. We are determined it will not manage us, or at least we choose to believe so. And thus, our attempts to numb pain, sustain a current behavior, maintain a desired course of action, or retain a relationship, and ultimately avoid discomfort—along with its accompanying consequences

– serve a need or fill a void. Even though we are in pain, we are unwilling to divest ourselves or are incapable of detaching ourselves from the behaviors or relationships supporting the pain. Let's take a look at an example of how this may show up in our lives.

Discomfort emerges from a myriad of behaviors, experiences, and relationships. However, individuals raised in highly abusive or dysfunctional families face an unusual challenge. Conflicted by the internal turmoil of their allegiances, many individuals desperately seek acceptance from their primary caregivers, staying in relationship with them although they continue to be injured by them. Although forms of parental abuse cover a broad area of violation, in my private practice I have witnessed a rise in the number of clients struggling with extreme discomfort emanating from a specific form of parental psychological abuse, Narcissistic Personality Disorder (NPD).

The word "narcissism" is thrown around quite a bit. And the truth is most individuals on occasion may embody narcissistic characteristics. Or, well-deserved pride over an achievement or quality may be perceived as "being better than anyone else." However, when someone is diagnosed with a personality disorder, it is serious because it embodies a more insidious nature. According to the *Diagnostic and Statistical Manual of Mental Disorders: Fifth Edition* (DSM-5), it is an "enduring pattern of inner experience or behavior" (DSM-5, p. 645). This pattern of behavior is inflexible, pervasive, and unrepresentative of one's cultural expectations. Personality disorders usually begin to emerge in adolescence and over time, cause significant distress in one's life. Narcissistic Personality Disorder (NPD) has many features. It is commonly characterized by an individual's grandiose sense of self-importance, a belief of superiority over others, a need for excessive admiration, and a general lack of empathy for others (DSM-5, p.671). For our discussion, it is important to note that the critical, judgmental, and reactive nature of adults with NPD is a defense against their own feelings of inadequacy. Rather than feeling shame, they are likely to shame or blame others. And, in order to get their own needs met, they use others.

Because their narcissistic parents' or guardians' needs supersede their children's, victims of NPD parents experience a great deal of self-loathing. After being harshly criticized for most of their lives and not measuring up to their parents' expectations, many individuals struggle with developing their own identity. In some cases, deeply damaged individuals begin to question their right to exist. And yet, even as adults, these injured beings find it difficult to detach themselves from their parents, guardians, or those entrusted with their wellbeing, who have proven unworthy of the adult child's trust or love. For many, it is important to be a part of a family, even if it is unsafe and unhealthy. For some, it is all they know.

One client, Alexandra, whom I worked with briefly over ten years ago and who has recently returned to therapy, is still attempting to prove herself to her narcissistic father. Although Alexandra is an accomplished professional with advanced degrees, she struggles with unrelenting shame and blames herself for not measuring up, being enough, or producing enough. Time and time again, she is at her father's beck and call, all in a futile attempt to have him "see her" and validate her. Each and every time Alexandra is in her father's presence, she is reinjured by his cruel judgment and harsh criticism. Although Alexandra suffers from an eating disorder, anxiety, and feels completely unlovable, she chooses not to detach herself from her father and from the abusive environment in which she was raised. Alexandra's discomfort controls her. She is not controlling it. As Alexandra continues to deafen herself from the calls of discomfort, her seeds of change remain dormant, asleep in their insulated womb.

For countless others, the unsettling and unwelcome emotion of discomfort can serve us in an entirely different way, only if certain conditions are met. From the stories of "A SHIFT In My Life" and from clients' narratives, we observe how there must be several specific conditions present within the contextual setting of discomfort in order for a call to be heard—when A SHIFT Is Awakened.

The conditions are threefold. The first two will be discussed together, as they are closely connected. However, depending on the unique circumstances of each person's experience, their order of presentation may vary.

- One condition is the following: we realize and accept we no longer are able to manage our discomfort.

- A second condition is as important: we have come to realize and accept the discomfort is managing us.

There are countless scenarios when these two conditions present themselves in our lives. For some, it is one in which a current way of being is no longer tolerable. We are distraught and disillusioned. We are going through the motions, but we are wondering what our purpose is and how to find more meaning in our lives.

For others of us, with this kind of disturbance, the degree of disruption we are experiencing shakes our core, dislodging support systems and shattering presenting beliefs and values. This leaves us feeling exposed, vulnerable, and at times, immobilized and unable to function. And as I have witnessed time and time again within therapeutic settings, it is the kind of disequilibrium that embodies an intense uncertainty causing us to question our current state of being, or what is left of it and us.

- The third condition essential to the awakening process, in which a call is heard, is the presence of a trigger or triggers.

Triggers are a form of psychological messaging, where our minds are forced to face and wrestle with intense emotions, feelings, and at times suppressed memories. Triggers come from anyone or anything—sights, sounds, smells, tactile objects, environmental cues, things people say—and the list goes on. Triggers can be layered and complex, or sometimes they are quite simple and straightforward.

Triggers may be internal or external, or both. They may show themselves in subtle, less invasive ways. Or they may present in sharper, disturbingly painful ways. A trigger may surface once or multiple times. Numerous triggers may attack a person's sense of wellbeing, chronically or episodically over long periods of time.

When a trigger/s is blended together with an acceptance of both our lack of control over our discomfort and its management of us, A SHIFT Is Awakened.

In Naomi's story from "A SHIFT In My Life," we observe how her seeds were awakened by her discomfort and its messenger—a sharp, acute trigger.

> In mid-2008, our country was entering into a recession. At the same time, my life was in a downward spiral. As a wife of thirty years and Mom of three children, I found myself navigating in unchartered waters. Our youngest daughter had graduated from college in 2007 and moved to New York to pursue her dreams of becoming an investment banker. My husband was enjoying his career, and our older daughter was married, living in Georgia. Our son was thriving in his career. After closing the door on a twenty-year job as a legal assistant, I was left to ponder what was next for me. This was supposed to be my time and I was curious about a whole new world of opportunities. After a lifetime of putting everyone else's needs first, I was looking forward to starting a path of self-growth, spiritual growth, and rediscovering who I really was and what my purpose was. However, I was not prepared for the tsunami coming my way.

In the summer of 2008, tensions within my family began to escalate as my youngest daughter was immersed in a very dark and toxic relationship. We had always been very close in our mother-daughter relationship; however, I felt her slipping away. Because the recession affected her ability to sustain a living in New York, my husband and I encouraged her to move back home. Initially she agreed but then changed her mind.

Several months passed. We received a phone call from one of her co-workers who shared that our daughter was getting involved with drug use. As she continued to resist our assistance to leave her destructive environment, I realized I could not help my daughter. The sting of despair and helplessness pierced my core. After always putting everyone else's needs before mine, I had to help me.

Naomi's story captures the process of awakening beautifully. As she embarked on a journey of self-exploration, she entered into a season of her life where she was prepared to experience some degree of distress. Her plans were derailed when her daughter's wellbeing was in jeopardy. Naomi leaned into her old self, returning to her role of *Mom* and "putting everyone's needs before mine [her own]." With the decline of her daughter's situation, Naomi entered into a state of disequilibrium where old ways of being no longer served a purpose in her life. Naomi recoiled, "The sting of despair and helplessness pierced my core." And yet, this painful trigger summoned her to a new way of being—"I had to help me."

Alexandra's story portrays how chronic discomfort sustains a way of being, although it continues to illicit reinjury and erode her sense of self. On the other hand, Naomi's story illustrates how a painful, acute state of disturbance and a piercing message from a trigger serve to awaken seeds of change.

And yet, there are times when we are not in extreme discomfort but we linger for long periods of time in a state of dissatisfaction or unease. We are aware of our unhappiness or discontent, but we choose to remain in our circumstances. During these periods of extended low-level distress, triggers or messengers may not present themselves overtly. Instead, they may show up more covertly over time.

Returning to Robert's story in A SHIFT Lies Dormant, we witness how Robert was groomed at a young age to take over his family's country club. After becoming quite successful with his future secure,

Robert's contentment was slowly dissipating as subtle messengers arose from within.

> By the mid-sixties, I had inklings that I did not want a future in food services, bar management, swimming pool maintenance, horses, harness racing, tennis, and public recreation. I was falling in love with education—not school—but learning and teaching.

Robert's "inklings" and his feelings—"falling in love with education"—slowly awakened his seeds. Robert did not allow his material comfort to camouflage his internal longings for a career change. Once his seeds were awakened, he began paying attention to them.

I have witnessed not only in my work with clients, but in my relationships with friends and family, how many individuals feel stuck or trapped in their professions, jobs, or careers. Yes, Robert had the advantage of financial means and family support. And while there may be social and economic restraints as well as personal responsibilities containing us in our discomfort, triggers are messaging us. Because triggers can be subtle, we just may not recognize them as such.

For example, each and every time we wish we were doing something else, or any time we envy another person's life, or whenever we make excuses or get angry at ourselves for our current state of being—we need to stop. We need to recognize these thoughts are messengers. They are calling us to awaken.

More importantly, each and every time we dismiss or ignore them, we sabotage another opportunity for an awakening and for growth. With each missed calling, we exile our seeds back into dormancy.

Aside from career or professional disenchantment, I often find relational discontent to be another area where individuals linger for very long periods of time. For a wide range of reasons, partners choose to manage their disturbances, often fearing the consequences of breaking off the relationship, separation, or divorce. Although it is very common for a trigger such as an affair, or abuse, or any kind of betrayal to awaken seeds and catapult a couple into a process of change, many times individuals suffer for years with internal triggers of unfulfillment, unworthiness, and feelings of unlovability.

Recently, I have been working with a forty-nine-year-old male client who is unhappy in his marriage. Because there are two young children, Phillip is committed to staying in the relationship. Although Phillip is the sole provider and an active father in his children's lives, he is constantly criticized and disrespected by his wife, and at times, his children. As we have been peeling away a few layers of camouflage, it has become clear that Phillip is extremely codependent.

There is much written about codependency, and the concepts around this personality trait are varied.

For our purposes, we will define codependency as an over-investment into someone, all in an attempt to rescue, control, or change a person and his behaviors. Phillip, like most codependents, is an extremely giving, caring, and compassionate person. At the same time, because he feels responsible for making his family happy, Phillip is quite controlling as he tries to fix, change, or manage their lives. When his family doesn't meet his expectations, or produce the results he desires, or if he doesn't feel appreciated, Phillip becomes angry, sad, and resentful. With his wife and children unchanged and unhappy, Phillip retreats for a while until another stressful situation surfaces. The pattern continues.

Working through his codependency, Phillip is starting to identify his unhealthy behaviors. He has begun letting go of his sense of over-responsibility and is learning how to establish healthy boundaries around his relationships with his wife and children. This has not been easy; however, Phillip is experiencing a modicum of relief and release from controlling others. By taking care of himself and investing into his wellness, Phillip is beginning to cultivate a sense of self-respect and self-love. As these new feelings begin to take hold, they in turn are acting as gentle messengers, slowly triggering an awakening of his eagerly awaiting seeds.

Just as there are those individuals who tolerate lower levels of discomfort for long periods of time, there are also those folks whose lives are ravaged with extreme levels of suffering for years. And yet, hope for an awakening is not lost forever on those who live in pain—facing hardships, fighting unwellness, numbing their unhappiness, and denying their origins.

After seasons of trying to manage the unmanageable, the unmanageable has a way of managing us. Our suffering intensifies as neglected layers of camouflage turn into mounds, weighing us down. Ironically, it is often this weightiness that forms a fissure within us, allowing triggers to break through the hardened layers of denial and creating an opening within our unknowing.

The Flower's journey portrays this kind of awakening. The blossom's tireless lifetime work of serving others professionally and personally continued to take its toll on her. In addition, horrific wounds from childhood through adulthood remained unhealed, bleeding internally and eroding her sense of self and sanity. With each season came the promise of a lighter way of being. But the Flower pushed on, her stem withered and weathered.

And then one day, the Flower was required to attend an all-day retreat at work. Exhausted from four twelve-hour shifts, she found her chair among the carefully structured circle. Seated directly across from the Flower sat her source of pain—a supervisor who had previously sexually harassed her. A report had been filed but nothing was done. The Flower felt his eyes scan her body. She lowered hers so as not to meet his.

The retreat began and the teachings were intense. The day was long and the Flower felt her armor weakening. When it came time for the Flower to share her insights into the topic, she felt the perpetrator's stare pierce her spirit. The Flower's voice shook, and then quaked. Her eyes looked up, blinded by the evil in his.

In that moment, a torrent of triggers pounded her soul. Flashbacks from childhood through adulthood of unwanted advances and horrific abuse flooded her mind. The overwhelm from the messengers sent the Flower into a psychological escape, where the image of her deceased grandmother surrounded her and protected her.

The Flower tried to stand, but she collapsed on the ground. She lay there, quiet and still. The words of an angel, disguised as a co-worker, messaged her softly, "It is time for you. Let me help." Underneath the thickened layers of camouflage, the Flower's buried seeds heard the call. A tiny crevice opened slightly and a thin layer of discomfort slid from within. The Flower stirred, as her seeds awakened.

Exercises—A SHIFT Is Awakened

In the middle phase of Winter Stillness, we begin to experience slight movement as A SHIFT Is Awakened. We learned we are awakened through a "calling," that signals us that our current way of being is no longer serving us well. Our calling emanates from a single source. That source is discomfort.

As you dig into A SHIFT Is Awakened, some questions may be difficult to answer. Take your time. If needed, pause and take a break. Then, keep going. This is your time. This is your path. Travel it bravely.

1. As you think about times of discomfort in your life, identify experiences you paid attention to and addressed. Describe what the discomfort was about and explain why you paid attention to it. Then, describe experiences where you did not pay attention and explain why you didn't.

2. In order for A SHIFT To Be Awakened, several conditions must be met. Read over the conditions listed below, and describe how a current shift is in the process of awakening or how it has awakened. Describe in detail how the conditions apply to you, what triggers messaged you, and how they are playing out in your life.

    ➤ First condition: I realize and accept that I no longer am able to manage my discomfort.

    ➤ Second condition: I have come to realize and accept the discomfort is managing me.

    ➤ Third condition: There is the presence of a trigger or triggers. Remember, triggers are a form of psychological messaging where our minds are forced to face and wrestle with intense emotions, feelings, and at times suppressed memories around discomfort.

3. Reflect upon different times in your discomfort when you were receiving messages or triggers and you chose to minimize, dismiss, or ignore them. Or perhaps you made excuses or blamed others for the intensification of your discomfort. Perhaps this is happening now. Describe these experiences. It is important to

make ourselves aware of when and why we have sabotaged prior attempts at awakenings.

4. Perhaps, like the Flower, your discomfort has been intensifying over a number of years. There are many triggers messaging you but you are denying them or repressing them. Over time, your layers of camouflage are thickening and are weighing you down. You are feeling broken by them. As painful as this is to acknowledge, describe this experience and how it is awakening you now.

5. In A SHIFT Is Awakened, whose story resonated with you the most? Why?

3   A SHIFT Awaiting Attention

"The next time you sense a strong emotion, take
some time to put a finger on what you're feeling. Get
quiet, turn inward, and just listen."

Lisa Nichols

During the early period of Winter Stillness, when A SHIFT Lies Dormant,
we learned when we are consumed in dealing with layers of camouflage,
our seeds of change remain in their dormancy and shielded from us. We
also learned how A SHIFT Is Awakened, as we enter into a middle phase
of Winter Stillness, a state of discomfort. First, we no longer are able to
manage our lives. Second, discomfort continues to dictate the course of
our lives. When our dormant seeds are awakened, it is because of our
acceptance of these two conditions along with the role of triggers,
messaging us through powerful unsettling emotions, feelings, and
memories.

As we are being awakened, these psychological messengers intensify
our distress. In order to mitigate their intrusion, our human reaction is to
turn our focus outward. Instead, our response must be just the opposite.

In the critical moments of our seeds awakening, we are being
summoned to assume an alternate mindset and posture. In this final phase
of Winter Stillness, we are being called to position ourselves inwardly for
A SHIFT Awaiting Attention. This is not easy. We have been conditioned
to do otherwise.

In today's culture and climate, we are messaged constantly to quantify
our worth by external measures. In our digital lives, our value is defined
by artificial and fleeting numbers of friends, followers, likes, and so on. In
our personal and professional lives, our success is determined largely
through attainment of material objects or possessions and through
achievement of status or title. In our efforts to sustain externally defined

worth and to avoid judgment, guilt, and shame, our focus remains outward. More importantly, in our need for external validation, we position ourselves in a posture contrary to personal shifts and to honoring the calling within.

In the stories of "A SHIFT In My Life" and in my work with clients, the posture required for A SHIFT Awaiting Attention is best described as that of a gardener. It is one who no longer desires to dominate or control circumstances, but is humbled by them. It is one who no longer is satisfied with fabricated or fleeting signs of growth, but who waits patiently for their authentic arrival. It is one who forfeits an external investment into a desired outcome and is willing to lean into an internal exploration of the unknown. And as is true of any purposeful gardener, the posture requires that one must carve out moments of stillness— essential pauses necessary for observation, assessment, and re-examination. The posture we assume must be one of intentional, inward positioning.

Returning to Margot's story, let's examine how she changed her posture, preparing for A SHIFT Awaiting Attention. After leaving her abusive family at seventeen, Margot lived with a friend's family. By age eighteen, she married her first real boyfriend. Margot's unhappiness carried over into her marriage, suffering from depression and isolation. After seventeen years of marriage and two children, Margot positioned herself for her call within.

> After several years of therapy with a godsend of a therapist, I finally divorced my husband. I was emotionally immature and let him have the children, although I loved them dearly.
>
> This was the first time I had ever lived alone. Doing so gave me some new self-confidence that I had never had. My shift began at this point, but wasn't fully developed until much later. Gone was the emotional abuse, judgment, and control from others on a daily basis.

Over the years as a therapist, I have listened to countless heartbreaking versions of Margot's story. However, I am moved by her courageous decision to live alone. By choosing to extract herself from "abuse, judgment, and control from others," she placed herself in a safe space tending to her healing. In doing so, Margot turned her attention inward, remaining quiet and still.

Sadly, it is all too common, especially with victims of chronic abuse or trauma, to remain in environments of chaos and confusion or to seek them out, unintentionally. It is what victims know. Because of their conditioning, they are drawn to what they are familiar with.

Jazmine's story from "A SHIFT In My Life," describes these conditions.

> When I was nineteen years old, I was living in Hollywood, working at a quasi-criminal place (massage parlor) in the mid 1970's. I was in an abusive relationship. Having left a family of origin of abuse, I was accustomed not to being treated well and not treating myself well either.

It takes strength to recognize that one's acceptance of unhealthiness is rooted in our own family patterns of dysfunction. Jazmine was able to do so by being brutally honest with herself—"Having left a family of origin of abuse, I was accustomed not to being treated well and not treating myself well either." And yet as Jazmine's story continues, just when her messengers of "intuition and probability" started to awaken her seeds, she abandoned them.

> Based on intuition and the probability of getting arrested and getting a record, I felt my time was running out. After engaging in a 12-Step program, I was beginning to form just a bit of self-esteem. I could feel a shift just starting to come on...
>
> In December 1974, I decided to escape the mess I was living in—my unhealthy relationship and dangerous work and lifestyle. I went to a recruiter's office to enlist in the military. With paper-work and dreams in hand, I went home to tell my alcoholic girlfriend. Although she was not happy, she agreed to attend Alcoholics Anonymous for a couple of months. I put my plans on hold and held on to the idea that if she just stopped drinking, all would be wonderful for us. Obviously, that was quite a fantasy.
>
> After a horrible experience at the massage parlor, where I felt deep disgust with myself, and an explosive argument with my partner that night, I once again resolved to escape and join Uncle Sam.

Jazmine's story depicts the relentless nature of disease and dysfunction. At the same time, it also illustrates the tenacity of her seeds, waiting for her discomfort to reach unmanageable levels and for her messengers of "...deep disgust..." and "...an explosive argument..." to bring about her awakening.

This time, at that critical moment of awakening, Jazmine paused and turned inward. Like a gardener taking time for observation, assessment, and re-examination, she quieted her mind and recalled honorable memories from generations past and their ensuing legacies. Her seeds once again lie awakened, eagerly Awaiting Attention.

> I remembered my mother saying how she regretted how she couldn't join the Waves for the Korean War. I remembered my two uncles who served in the Navy during World War II, and Uncle Bernard who survived being stationed on the Arizona at Pearl Harbor in 1942. I recalled my great-grandfather, a Civil War Veteran, and his self-portrait, which hung in a prominent spot in my grandparents' living room. I decided that I wanted more than anything else to belong, to be respected, and to escape the life I was living.

By being still and turning inward, Jazmine positioned herself to pay attention to her recollections. Humbled by their service to our country, Jazmine leaned into the memories of her ancestors while her seeds awakened fully, drawing strength and authenticity from them.

Both Jazmine's and Margot's stories illustrate how to assume an inward posture. We must not only be still and patient, but must also allow ourselves to be vulnerable. Whether it is in therapy, a 12 Step program, in a moment of defeat, or during a period of reckoning or recollection, we must be brave as we wrestle with behaviors, thoughts, and feelings—both unfamiliar and uncomfortable. It is in the soil of discomfort where seeds of change start to yawn and stretch, as they await our attention.

A couple of years ago, a strong, confident, highly successful middle-aged female came into therapy. After attending 12-Step meetings for a number of years, Suzanne wanted to work on some personal issues in a more private setting. Our sessions were productive; however, there were protective layers of camouflage preventing deeper exploration. I waited, building trust around our connection and keeping a pulse on Suzanne's levels of vulnerability. Over the months, Suzanne began to open up little by little. I moved slowly, giving her time to adjust to the suffering within her. I knew if a layer of camouflage was peeled away prematurely, Suzanne would withdraw. Bravely, she continued her work, but I felt there was more.

And then, one late Saturday afternoon, Suzanne entered my office like a little black kitten, fragile and frightened. Painfully, she disclosed how a male client had verbally "shamed" her, in a public professional setting. As I listened to her story and validated her courage, Suzanne curled up in the big brown leather chair across from me and cried. Tears streamed down her olive complexion, dripping from her chin. With her black long-sleeved shirt, she gently wiped them away. Again, I waited.

When her tears subsided, Suzanne spoke softly, "Holli, why would he say that to me? Do you think what he said is true? All I wanted to do was disappear."

Looking into Suzanne's eyes, I could feel her pain. Asking me these questions was hard. Peeling away this layer of camouflage was so excruciating for her. And yet, by making herself completely vulnerable, she leaned into an internal posture.

I responded gently, with questions. "Suzanne, have you ever been shamed publicly before? Can you remember a time when you felt this kind of pain—when you wanted to disappear?"

Suzanne's body uncurled itself from the chair's womb. She sat quietly, turning inward and scanning her memory. The fragility from moments before was replaced with intensity. Suzanne's eyes met mine. A trigger surfaced. She spoke.

"It's so painful to think about. It happened such a long time ago. I had forgotten about it until you asked me. Yes...I was publicly shamed when I was in high school. Something very private and very personal about me was displayed for everyone to see. It was the most humiliating and degrading thing that could ever happen to a person. And, no one stood up for me, not even my parents. No one did anything about it."

Suzanne took a breath and fought her way through the waves of uneasiness. She continued, "When that happened, I wanted to disappear...just like I did when my client shamed me."

I sat quietly as Suzanne remained still, paying attention to her calling. She paused and reflected on its significance.

"I have buried that horrible incident for years. I have not thought about it or talked of it. But I have always carried its shame. Holli, how do I get rid of it? How do I let it go?"

Suzanne's story illustrates two important components in the delicate beginnings of shifting.

First, it took quite a bit of time for Suzanne to feel comfortable and safe in our work together. I followed her pace and kept a pulse on her levels of strength and vulnerability. I knew when to push on the discomfort and when to back off. However, it was Suzanne who maintained the posture of a gardener, carefully tending to her wellbeing by investing into therapy week after week and bravely unearthing her feelings.

Second, when the trigger came into play—a male client shaming her publicly—she did not dismiss it or turn outward, embracing artificial releases for temporary comfort. This time, she again claimed her position as the gardener of her life, remaining quiet and still and risking emotional exposure. By turning inward, she was able to listen to her authentic calling, as we processed past pain and connected it to her present shame.

From the stories of "A SHIFT In My Life" and from the client stories I have shared as well as with my work with other clients, I believe it is imperative to allow for ample time to be still, turn inward, and to listen. I believe it is in those quiet, deeply reflective states where our attention has time to absorb the awakening of our seeds. Are there individuals who experience Ah-ha moments or wake-up calls that initiate the shifting process? Yes, of course there are. I'm just not confident that brief or passing experiences possess the organic nature critical to sustaining movement from dormancy to awakening during Winter Stillness.

In the late 1990s, I was completing my Master's Degree in Psychology. As part of my trainee hours, I worked at a large women's shelter in the bay area in California. Along with staffing the crisis phone lines, completing intakes and counseling women leaving abusive relationships and environments, I also had the privilege of co-facilitating a psycho-educational group for women who were living in a two-year transitional housing program. Through their hard work and commitment to their recovering, these women had earned placement in a semi-independent living program. Although there were rigid guidelines and protocol around their safety, the women were given limited access to various social activities.

One of the recommendations we strongly encouraged clients to follow, however, was to avoid dating or entering into relationships for at least one year. This was not to punish them. This recommendation was for one reason only—a rare opportunity for the women, offering them time to be still, turn inward, and to listen to their callings as they worked through their multitude of issues. Although there may have been one or two exceptions, those clients who rushed into relationships and who turned their focus outward were not successful in the program. Many left prematurely returning to their abusers or entering into unhealthy relationships. On the contrary, for those who made the commitment to stay the course of A SHIFT Awaiting Attention, they heard the call of their awakening seeds and listened to them.

In bringing this chapter of Winter Stillness to a close, it is important to recognize there are individuals who implement mindfulness routines, meditative practices, or spiritual rituals into their daily lives with the intention of positioning themselves in stillness. With practice and discipline, they embrace turning inward and become more acute listeners. Like seasoned gardeners, their attention has been conditioned to respond to their calls. Does this make their journeys less difficult? Not necessarily. However, it is often their openness to their calls and their timely attention to them that accelerate and accommodate their shifting process.

For those of us who do not routinely lean into an internal focus, it is always available to us. From the stories of "A SHIFT In My Life," we witness how differing states of discomfort are the impetus for individuals to pause and position themselves in order to be still, turn inward, and listen.

Returning to Britt's story in A SHIFT Lies Dormant, an unexpected illness drew her focus inward as she sought to discover the reasons "...why my gut was crying out to get my attention." In addition to following her doctor's three-pronged approach, Britt also intentionally set aside time for internal posturing.

> I followed my doctor's instructions by taking medication and controlling my diet. I took a regimen of homeopathic supplements to enhance gut health. Most germane to this time in my life, I began a twice daily practice of meditation followed by visualization. I opened my mind and went nosing around to find the underlying cause of my disease.
>
> Stress and genetics were two simple explanations. However, I wanted to identify the behaviors that had led me to this critical juncture, and figure out how to make a significant shift to return to health and balance.

Britt's story beautifully illustrates one of the most important facets of turning inward and paying attention to our awakening seeds. Her "twice daily practice of meditation followed by visualization" were instrumental to her process. As Britt describes, "I opened my mind and went nosing around..." When we quiet the noise around us, we take on the purposeful role of a gardener as we lean into internal exploration of the unknown. And when we let go of predetermined outcomes, we open our minds to all kinds of possibilities for growth.

Whether times of stillness are imposed upon us, or we periodically invite them in, or we have incorporated them into our daily practices, our awakening seeds will await our attention. Sometimes, we are positioned to hear their call and we pay attention to them. Sometimes, we don't. Consequently, our seeds become impatient and return to their dormancy, until another wave of disturbance and its messengers call for their awakening. Or sometimes, extreme levels of suffering along with powerful messengers jolt seeds out of their slumber and force an awakening, pulling us inward and demanding our attention.

The Flower who floundered and then fell to the ground did not choose her stillness. Her seeds were awakened by dense mounds of discomfort and piercing triggers filled with flashbacks of abuse. Weighted down by a lifetime of cruelty and with present-day violations unearthing past unhealed wounds, the paralyzed Flower surrendered to her circumstances. Unable to perform her professional duties to the required standard, the shame-filled Flower accepted an unwanted gift from her place of employment—time to be still.

When the Flower reached out to me through a phone call, her voice was shaky. She sounded parched, and her words sort of choked from her stem in short broken bursts. In her pain, she described how her purpose, her profession for helping others, had been stripped from her. She was completely raw and vulnerable. She was frightened and fearful.

I listened. I reflected her pain. I let her know I heard her and understood. And then I gently asked the Flower, "Are you willing to take this time of stillness to turn inward and to listen to the callings awaiting your attention and that have brought you here?"

Her cries of despair came through the call, breaking the silence. The Flower's words flowed from a well of tears. "I am lost with nowhere to go. Although I am afraid, I am willing."

Exercises—A SHIFT Awaiting Attention

Entering into the final phase of Winter Stillness, we learned that when we are in our discomfort, it is our tendency to turn our focus outward. We are drawn to external forms of validation to assuage our uneasiness. We are also conditioned to suppress or numb our discomfort through various unhealthy or harmful behaviors or relationships. Sometimes, we choose a diversion that may be healthy but it is one that sustains an outward focus. Our challenge in A SHIFT Awaiting Attention is to turn our focus inward. This is not easy. We have been conditioned to do otherwise.

As you dive into A SHIFT Awaiting Attention, some questions may be difficult to answer. Take your time. If needed, pause and take a break. Then, keep going and growing. Trust the process and your path.

1. Reflecting back on your experiences of discomfort, describe where your focus is directed. Where do you turn? What do you do? How does it help you, at least in the short term? How does it hurt you, with the long-term goal of changing and growing?

2. In the stories from "A SHIFT In my Life" and from clients' narratives, we learned how several individuals already implemented practices such as praying, meditating, or other mindful exercises in order to turn inward and begin paying attention to their awakenings. Others sought our resources such as counseling in order to assume a posture of intentionally turning inward.

   When you are called to pay attention to your discomfort, describe what you are already practicing and how it is beneficial to you. Or, describe what you are willing to implement into your routine so that you take on a posture of being still, listening, observing and examining your awakening shift.

3. If you have been living in discomfort for a long period of time, identify and describe what external sources of conditioning are contributing to sustaining this discomfort. Although there may be others, this includes issues such as codependent behaviors, unhealthy relationships, financial pressures, family dynamics, and so on. This difficult area is extremely important to explore.

4. As you practice turning inward, you may begin to feel extremely vulnerable. This is very natural. In the stories from *SHIFTING Bravely*, we witnessed how many individuals felt shamed,

uncertain, and unsafe. Although these feelings are uncomfortable, it is important you acknowledge them. While you are turning inward, identify and describe what feelings are coming up for you. Explain what is behind them.

5. Not only must you be willing to turn inward in order to pay attention to your awakening seeds, but you must also give yourself ample time. Like a gardener, you must be patient. Identify and describe experiences in your life when you invested lengthy periods of time in discovering what you are being called to do. What was that like for you? What did you learn? And, what are you currently willing to commit to?

6. In A SHIFT Awaiting Attention, whose experience spoke to you? Why?

Season Two: Spring Stirrings

4   A SHIFT Takes Root

"It takes time for the seeds to begin growing within,
time to understand and process…"

                                         Bryant Gill

The first phase of Winter Stillness is a time of rest for our seeds. We have come to understand that during a period of dormancy, our seeds wait patiently while we are busy tending to our lives. During the middle phase of Winter Stillness, we learned how our seeds are awakened out of their deep winter slumber, when timely messengers trigger unmanageable discomfort or uncontrollable disturbance. And, during the final phase, we have learned the significance of Winter Stillness in our lives, as we take time to turn inward and pay attention to the calling of our seeds.

As we enter into the season of Spring, we do so with anticipation and hope. We have broken through the camouflage of unknowing and become aware of possibilities for change. Longing for Spring Stirrings, we feel excitement as well as uncertainty. In *SHIFTING Bravely,* we must continue to embrace the mindset of a gardener, "It takes time for seeds to begin growing within, time to understand and process…"(Gill). Specific conditions must be met "…for seeds to begin growing within."

- Preparation of the soil

- Assessment of the soil's environment

Let's take a look at how these apply to our seasonal process of self-growth, when A SHIFT Takes Root.

Most clients reach out for therapy when they have had an awakening. Although they may be confused, depressed, frightened, or ashamed, they are listening to their calls of discomfort or disturbance. Some are in a posture of focusing inward and paying attention, while others have difficulty doing so—especially in the beginnings of their awakenings. For many individuals, their soil is filled with toxins of guilt, self-blame, shame, and secrecy.

These toxic particles are like blocks of hardened clay, acting as barriers against the process of germination where roots reach into the earth while stems begin to stretch upward. The beginnings of growth will be stunted or sabotaged if the roots cannot move through porous soil in order to access water for nourishment. Thus, in order for a seed to begin growing within, it is necessary for most individuals to spend as much time as needed in order to examine their internal conditions for growth. By sifting and sorting through the debris in our soil, we are cleaning out unhealthy inhibitors and clearing the way for the first phase of Spring Stirrings.

Returning to Suzanne's story in A SHIFT Awaiting Attention, after several months of therapy she disclosed a painful episode of public shaming at her place of work. Responding to a few carefully guided questions, Suzanne was able to connect her present pain to a horrific episode of public shaming when she was a teenager. In her words, she described how this incident poisoned her soil, "I have buried that incident for years. I have not thought about it or talked about it. But I have always carried it with me."

And then, Suzanne added, "Holli, how do I address it? How do I let it go?"

Over the next several months, Suzanne bravely unearthed the debris of injustice within her. As she identified each particle of injury, she realized how the public shaming experienced as a teen set her on a course of self-loathing and self-destruction. In one of our sessions, she bravely disclosed the accumulation of pain.

> For years after the incident, I was bullied at school. I was called filthy names...just disgusting and degrading stuff. They attacked my religion, my identity as a female, and even my name. And, I still can't get over it today as I think about how my parents brushed it off. My dad told me to suck it up...to get over it.
>
> Things got so bad that I started drinking. I had to do something. I hated myself so much and I couldn't tolerate it. It was my only way to escape...and to numb my shame.

During our sessions, Suzanne continued to sift through her sources of debris and to remove them through meaningful processes of releasing. She often leaned on her 12 Step program along with spiritual practices, which provided avenues for letting go. As her soil began to take on a porous texture, she surprised me one day with another piece of self-examination.

"Remember how I told you I wanted to disappear after the shaming attacks? Well, I realized that ever since the incident in high school, I started wearing all black clothes and dressing like a guy. I didn't want to be noticed. I didn't want to look feminine. And, I'm still doing it today."

I'll never forget that session. For the first time in almost a year, a stunning, petite black feline sat large in the big brown leather chair, which previously had swallowed her up. Her torso was erect but elegant, her long arms poised comfortably on the side rests, and her slender legs crossed in a confident pose, like a cat in charge of the room.

Her beautiful smile radiated the space between us. Suzanne's voice was strong, "I feel like I am starting to understand who I really am."

Suzanne's story clearly illustrates the importance of examination of past and present wounds, but it also demonstrates the crucial process of their removal and their release. When we take time to turn inward, flush out poisonous particles, and tend to our internal healing, we are also preparing our soil for growth. In Suzanne's words, we see how her awareness—"I am starting to understand who I really am"—is clearing the way for her seeds to begin growing within.

In Chapter One, A SHIFT Lies Dormant, we explored how numerous forms of camouflage contain us in our state of unknowing. One of the many common forces blocking our awareness is the interference of life messages, especially those that are destructive and self-deprecating. These harmful life messages clog our soil, working against the conditions necessary for when A SHIFT Takes Root.

Returning to Britt's story from A SHIFT Awaiting Attention, we recall how she was experiencing tremendous success in her professional career as an educator and also thriving as a mother of two sons and a loving partner to her husband. And yet, she was suffering physically with undiagnosed "gut issues." In her search for answers and direction, she began turning inward, implementing "twice daily practices of meditation followed by visualization." As Britt's story continues, we witness how she tended to her soil through careful examination followed by mindful preparation.

> One day, through my meditative practice, I became acutely aware how I had a lot of angst about failure and that my anxiety resided primarily in my gut. I asked myself, why?
>
> I continued to look for clues in my upbringing and was finally struck by the realization that both my mother and my older sister

had instilled in me, from the time I was small, a belief that I was inept and would fail at anything I tried. The life message I began believing was that only with their help and their strong hand could I overcome this deficiency and find some modicum of success in my undertakings. They could rescue me from my inadequacies, if I would let them take over and manage what was needed to succeed.

Now that I was a grown woman, I realized how I had believed their messages and carried within myself a strong mindset that feared failure at every turn. Without realizing it, I had carried this childhood message for all my life. It led to an assumption, a deep inner belief, that I was bound to screw up my every undertaking. I was burdened with this unending fear of failure. Couple that with a desire for achievement and perfection (also a false life script), it was no surprise I ended up with gut issues.

Britt's story powerfully portrays the impact of shameful life messages on our souls. The more we internalize them as our truths, the more we contaminate our soil. Britt's words speak to their impact upon her—"It led to an assumption, a deep inner belief, that I was bound to screw up my everyday undertaking." In addition, Britt carried within her a "false life script." Similar to a life message, Britt's identification of her sister and mother being the only ones who "could rescue me from my inadequacies, fueled her desire for perfection" and filled her soil with more toxins. And yet, she bravely continued to explore their impact, taking time to understand and process, while gently preparing her soil for growth.

Once I focused on this realization, I took time to review my performance to date. Hmmmmm, I not only succeeded at most things I did, I excelled. So, what the heck? Then it struck me. This early messaging was not really about me, even though it affected me deeply. This was about my mother and older sister's need to feel in control and empowered. Yes, I provided a convenient ongoing opportunity.

I realized it was "they" who needed to build their own self-image by "rescuing" me because clearly, in their minds, they knew what had to be done and how to do it. It enabled them to feel good about themselves at my expense. Because of these old messages, my every undertaking had become a struggle to overcome the inner voices that spoke to me of failure and caused significant anxiety.

Once I knew what to look for, I could see the pattern in my relationships with my mother and my older sister, both past and present. It has taken me many years to acknowledge that inner voice and disempower it.

There are two very important takeaways from Britt's story in "A SHIFT In My Life." First, there was no indication in her story that Britt partook in any kind of formal therapy or counseling. However, this does not diminish in any way her focused commitment into an internal exploration of her soil. By tapping into her meditative practices, Britt was able to challenge her beliefs and clear her mind of faulty thinking. Through her periods of reflection, her realizations led her to prepare her soil by discarding old life messages while entertaining healthy new messages: "This early messaging was not really about me, even though it affected me deeply. This was about my mother and older sister's need to feel in control and empowered."

The second takeaway is also critical. Britt continued her hard work of examination, understanding how her years of shame-filled life messages impacted her greatly: "Because of these old messages, my every undertaking had become a struggle to overcome the inner voices that spoke to me of failure and caused significant anxiety." She did not give up or give in to them. She realized, preparing her soil was not a one and done practice. Because her particles of toxic debris were deeply embedded, the cleansing of her soil would be an ongoing process: "I could see the pattern in my relationships with my mother and my older sister, both past and present. It has taken me many years to acknowledge that inner voice and disempower it."

It is important to remember how gardeners spend a great deal of time examining and preparing their soil. Even after seeds have been planted, gardeners remain mindful of the soil's constitution and condition. Like a dedicated gardener, Britt understood how her soil required consistent attention, not just in the examination and preparation phase, but throughout her seasonal process of self-growth.

As A SHIFT Takes Root, understanding the condition of our soil gives each of us permission to move at our own pace and to trust our own process. Where there has been much damage, much will be required of us as we continue SHIFTING Bravely. Gleaning from lessons within stories of "A SHIFT In My Life," there is evidence that initial subtle growth of roots may start to form during A SHIFT Awaiting Attention, even in the presence of the deeply damaged conditions. Two stories, from patient purposeful gardeners Margot and Jazmine, spoke of utilizing their periods of turning inward and paying attention to their awakenings as a time of reflection and increased self-awareness. Doing so enabled them to transition naturally into their processes of examination and preparation.

Returning to Margot's story and invoking her own words, we recall how after divorcing her husband and choosing to live alone, Margot was free from "the emotional abuse, judgment, and control from others on a daily basis." Through honest, thorough examination of her soil, Margot was able to identify toxic debris restricting her beginnings of growth.

> After years of adjusting to independence, I was still mostly unhappy and depressed, although some antidepressants had taken the edge off of the depression. My previous life haunted me and I couldn't break out of old, negative self-talk. I finally became miserable enough and determined enough to make some new changes.

Margot's story illustrates several important pieces in her process of internal examination. First, she did not rush the process—"after years of adjusting to independence"—and secondly, she tended to her mental health—"some antidepressants had taken the edge off of the depression." Most importantly, Margot was able to identify how her unhealthy soil continued to contaminate her present condition—"My previous life haunted me and I couldn't break out of old, negative self-talk."

From Jazmine's story in Chapter Three, we learned how she utilized her time turning inward and paying attention to her seeds' callings by reflecting on her ancestors' service in the military. These recollections proved to be a powerful force in moving her into Spring Stirrings. However, it was an unexpected pause in her process that contributed to the conditioning of her soil.

> I quit my lucrative job as a dominatrix, changed my attitude about the Vietnam War, filled out the application to enlist in the U.S. Army and announced my intentions to marry Uncle Sam. I was entered in the "delayed entry program," so I had to sit around for a couple more months.
>
> The delay only deepened my resolve.

Jazmine's story illustrates two very important lessons in transitioning from A SHIFT Awaiting Attention to A SHIFT Takes Root. First, as we are paying attention to our callings and taking care of our immediate wellbeing, we may need to make decisions and start making changes. Jazmine did just that by quitting her previous job, applying to the Army, and starting out on a new career. In addition, there was an unexpected pause—"I was entered into the 'delayed entry program,' so I had to sit around for a couple of months." This imposed pause forced her to examine her soil thoroughly, clearing it for growth—"The delay only deepened my resolve."

For both Margot and Jazmine, it is important to note how even though they began their internal examinations of their soil during A SHIFT Awaiting Attention, they maintained a steady and strong commitment to removing toxic debris and creating healthier conditions for growth.

For those of us whose soil has not been as riddled with clumps of contagion, the examination and preparation phase may lend itself to a smoother, less intense transition from paying attention to their awakening seeds to experiencing their seeds growing within.

Robert's story from "A SHIFT In My Life" is uniquely illustrative of this. In Chapter Two, A SHIFT Is Awakened, we learned how Robert's childhood and young adult life was filled with rich experiences and diverse opportunities within his family's business. After paying attention to his awakening seeds—having "inklings" of dissatisfaction with his current choice of career and "falling in love with education"—Robert's soil was well-conditioned for growth. While Robert continued to pursue his dreams focusing on experiential and interdisciplinary programs for kids, he respectfully acknowledged his parents' sacrifice and support while staying true to his self-growth.

> My parents had everything tied-up in the land and club. They were doing all they could to support my dreams. Freeing my folks gave me an excuse to decide what I really wanted to do with my life.

Although Robert's story is an example of a less encumbered process of when A SHIFT Takes Root, it is important to acknowledge that life-changing decisions were made by Robert's parents and by him. These decisions greatly impacted their futures. However, like a masterful gardener, Robert's careful tending to the decision-making process enriched his soil, easing his seeds into a strategic position for growth.

As we have learned from the stories in "A SHIFT In My Life" and from clients, once we have heard the calling of our seeds awakening and we are paying attention to them, we want to provide them with soil in which A SHIFT Takes Root. Doing so may require investing significant time in order to increase understanding of our soil's condition and assuring ample time for internal examination and processing. Or, we may find that our soil has been naturally enriched by beneficial sources of influence and nurturance. Either way, it is important to assess one final condition of our soil—its environment.

In conducting a bit of investigation on the growing process of seeds, I discovered there is a plethora of different kinds of soil, tailored to the various types of crops, plants, flowers, and so on. One of the most commonly used types of soil consists of a rich, sandy loam (a combination of sand, silt, and clay). Compost, a mixture of nutrients, is frequently inserted as a source of enrichment. In readying seeds for germination, the soil should be of correct ratios of soil types with the intent of achieving the right consistency and texture.

Not only is it necessary to have a healthy balanced composition of soil, but the growth environment must meet certain requirements as well. When A SHIFT Takes Root, a seed needs the soil to be damp, warm, and dark. The first signs of germination consist of the main root and stem. It is essential for roots to have access to water. By keeping the soil damp, the roots absorb the water, receiving their nourishment while also feeding the stem. The warmth of the soil and surrounding darkness provide protection for the seed, supplying chemical energy necessary for the making of new cells and safeguarding it for continual growth.

In readying ourselves for Spring Stirrings, we must also take an honest assessment of our growth environments. Although no environment is perfect, we can create spaces to provide strength and support for the beginnings of growth. In the stories from "A SHIFT In My Life," we witnessed how Margot and Jazmine left their unhealthy surroundings by moving away. In Suzanne's story, we saw how the therapeutic process provided a safe warm space for her roots to begin growing. In Britt and Robert's stories, we learned how Britt's adult environment and Robert's childhood and young adulthood environment were enriched with family support, enabling their roots to descend as their stems began to stretch upward.

In my work as a therapist, I have found when growth environments are dysfunctional, damaging, or dangerous, it is not impossible for growth to take root but it is extremely difficult. Although there are many reasons for this, several are worth noting. First, during the initial phase of Spring Stirrings, an individual's identity, worth, and sense of belonging are often weakened or fractured. As change is being considered, fragile individuals who are unable to tether themselves to environments that are enriching and supportive, become frightened and overwhelmed in the early stages of growth. Often feeling unworthy of change, they abandon their process of self-growth before it can take hold.

Second, toxic and dysfunctional family relationships are resistant to change, especially if they have been in place for long periods of time. Consequently, with an unhealthy environment working to keep the status quo, any minor spurt of growth is often challenged or resisted by destructive rules or damaging norms. Thus, it feels safer for individuals to succumb to their former states of being and their roles within their environments rather than stand up to or against opposition.

Lastly, without a safe environment or a protected space for growth to take root, it is difficult for individuals to experience internal nourishing elements of resilience or perseverance. The energy needed to do so is nonexistent. The internal fuel source required to provide strength and stamina to begin self-growth is simply not available. It is like expecting a seed, that has awakened and whose calls have been heard, to begin growing without water and without the essential protective properties of warmth and of darkness.

As A SHIFT Takes Root, we have learned the importance of examining and preparing healthy conditions for our soil as well as conducting an honest assessment of its environment. We learned, "It takes time for seeds to begin growing within, time to understand and process" (Gill). The Flower who found her way into my office was no different.

Watching the fragile Flower make her way slowly and cautiously up five concrete steps leading to the office building door, I couldn't help but wonder about the conditions of her soil, and if her awakened seeds were searching for water and a nourishing environment of warmth and darkness. With her stem slightly bent over and her eyes facing downward, she balanced herself on the steel railing provided.

Greeting the Flower at the front door and welcoming her into my office, I noted her graceful cadence as she flowed into the room. She continued looking downward and whispered, *Hello.* She cautiously positioned herself in the large brown leather chair, quickly scanning the surroundings while assessing its safety. Reaching into her small crocheted purse to retrieve her pen, her hands shook slightly as she made out her check. I stood to thank her and receive the check, along with additional paperwork she had brought.

The Flower adjusted her long silky summer dress to cover her legs and straightened her lace shawl around her shoulders. With her hands poised in her lap, she closed her eyes and took in a deep breath. I waited until the Flower was settled, sensing her need for time. After reviewing a few of the ethical and legal issues within the paperwork, I gently asked her if she felt ready. The Flower nodded. I began.

"Thank you so much for being here today. Thank you for the courage to call, to reach out, and to begin this process. We spoke a little last time over the phone about what has brought you here. I'd like to hear more...whenever you are ready and whatever you feel comfortable sharing."

During our first session and every week thereafter over the next five months, the Flower courageously and painfully opened up and allowed the callings of her awakenings to come pouring out. Her soil was filled with hard black clay: toxic blocks of sexual traumas, other forms of childhood and adult physical and psychological abuse, years of neglect and scarcity, and chronic horrific betrayals from persons of faith as well as family.

Following her pace and providing her with tools for self-care and self-regulation throughout the unearthing of deeply embedded injuries and injustices, we began clearing out her old mangled roots of shame, self-blame, and self-hatred. Many times, we would begin cleaning out scar tissue disguised as debris when another tsunami of emotional toxins surfaced. Keeping a pulse on her strength and stamina, I would often pause and move into mindful or meditative exercises to calm and re-center the fractured Flower.

With her agreement, the Flower and I sought out a well-respected psychiatrist who assessed, diagnosed, and treated her for Major Depressive Disorder and Posttraumatic Stress Disorder. He also helped her with anxiety and sleep issues, especially as we worked through her past trauma and abuse. Most importantly, this physician provided additional compassionate support as well as securing a safety net around the Flower's wellbeing.

Over time, the Flower's trust in herself, in the process, and in me grew. She no longer looked away, but allowed her eyes to find safety in mine. Her voice strengthened from a whisper, but always maintained the flow of a song. During the most difficult phases of examination and preparation of her soil, the Flower turned inward, embracing her ancestral indigenous spiritual beliefs for connection and protection. Being able to utilize them in our process together provided the Flower with a source of ongoing support and strength.

For the first few months of our work together, the Flower lived alone in a remote area. Because of irregular dangerous activity near her house, she was constantly triggered and frightened. This hazardous environment, of course, undermined and at times arrested her internal exploration. With the help of a friend who expedited the process, the Flower was able to locate and move to a more safe and secure home. I remember her words a few weeks after she was settled.

"Holli, I didn't realize how nervous and scared I was. As soon as my dogs would start barking, I would jump out of bed, check all the doors, windows, then lock my bedroom door and blockade myself in my room. I was terrorized…and I couldn't sleep…"

She paused. "Now, I feel completely safe. And, I have a few neighbors who are friendly and we watch out for each other."

She smiled and added, "Oh my dogs are still with me… I'm not sleepin' anywhere without them. They'll let me know if someone or some critter is out there!"

As our time together was moving into its sixth month, the Flower bravely continued to examine and prepare her soil. With much to unearth, much time was needed. Her new healthy environment was also contributing to her readiness, when A SHIFT Takes Root.

And then one Saturday morning as she drove up to the office for her session, I noticed the Flower was not alone. A tall slender strong male exited the car, hurried over to the passenger's side, and helped the Flower out. With his hand under her arm, he guided the delicate Flower up the stairs and delivered her to the door.

Opening the main door, I smiled and greeted them both. The Flower beamed and introduced her "man."

The sturdy slender, soft-spoken "man" lowered his head and whispered, "It's nice to meet you, Holli."

Like a long trunk of a silver Birch tree searching for anonymity, his body leaned a bit closer to the Flower while his eyes remained glued to the ground. I offered the tender Birch a seat in the large waiting room, but he declined and walked briskly to the car.

When the Flower and I were seated and ready to begin, she spoke softly.

"I met my 'man' a couple of months ago. He's really good to me…but he's shy." And then she spoke with sadness in her voice. He's not good with people."

During our session, the lovely Flower opened more fully, revealing a tenderness and a vulnerability around her relationship. When she spoke of her "man," the Flower shared he had suffered much in his life, as she had. She wanted me to know she was "taking things slowly" and she "felt safe with him."

After our session concluded, I walked the Flower to the office building front doors. The long silver Birch waited at the bottom of the steps. Seeing her, he rushed up to the top, taking her hand and guiding her to the car.

Watching as they walked hand in hand, I wondered how this relationship would impact the Flower, her soil's condition, and her environment.

As the Flower's seeds began growing within, would it bring contagion?

Or would it offer the nourishment of water and the protective properties of warmth and darkness? Only time would tell as the Flower continued *SHIFTING Bravely*.

Exercises—A SHIFT Takes Root

Entering into the first phase of Spring Stirrings, we leaned into more sensitive and tender areas of *SHIFTING Bravely*. This is a critical phase of deeper examination of ourselves and our environments. In many of the stories, individuals sought out professional guidance, counseling, or support groups in order to navigate this part of their journey. Some tapped into other sources of spiritual support and mindfulness practices.

Perhaps you have as well. Or perhaps, doing so may benefit you. Regardless, some questions may be difficult to answer. Take your time. If needed, pause and take a break. Then, keep growing and healing. Your path is unique to you. It is calling you to be brave.

1. In the first part of Chapter Four, we learned the importance of examining our "soil" and clearing out toxic debris. These destructive particles have formed within us as a result of childhood wounds, trauma, or abuse. It is also shows up in shaming life messages that emanate from any and all kinds of adverse life experiences. As you begin to dig really deep and examine your "soil," identify and describe any debris that may be interfering with your shift taking root.

2. We witnessed in *SHIFTING Bravely* how the process of examining soil played out very differently for each individual story. We learned, "Where there is much damage, much will be required of us." If you have already invested into a process for doing this hard work, describe your experience and how it impacted your growth. If you have not done so, what are you willing to commit to?

3. If your "soil" has not been contaminated with toxic debris but there are still life experiences holding you back, describe and explain them. Then, identify what steps you will take in order to cultivate healthier conditions for your growth.

4. Perhaps, similar to Robert's story, your "soil" is enriched by your life experiences and lends itself to a smooth transition into your shift. Describe and explain your experience.

5. In the second part of Chapter Four, we learned the importance of assessing our growth environments and how they are impacting our emergence. As you think about your shift beginning to take

root, describe your environment/s and how they are contributing to or hindering your growing process. If they are hindering your process, identify what steps you will take in order to cultivate healthier environments for your growth.

6. Whose story in A SHIFT Takes Root are you connecting with more closely? Why?

5   A SHIFT Emerges

"For a seed to achieve its greatest expression, it must come completely undone. The shell cracks, its insides come out and everything changes."

Cynthia Occelli

During Winter Stillness, we moved through three phases: our sleepy seeds enjoyed a time of slumber; they were awakened by calls of discomfort; and, they were quietly surprised when met with some long-awaited attention. With hope and anticipation, our seeds welcomed Spring Stirrings—signs of movement and potential growth. In the first phase of Spring, we learned how A SHIFT Takes Root. We have come to understand, "It takes time for seeds to begin growing within, time to understand and process" (Gill). In order to initiate a healthy beginning, we learned the importance of becoming aware of and understanding the conditions of our soil. We explored a three-part process—examination, preparation, and assessment—and its vital role in a seasonal process of self-growth.

In the stories from "A SHIFT In My Life" as well as clients' stories, we witnessed the commitment and courage it takes to conduct an internal examination of one's soil as well as to embrace the focused tasks of removing and releasing toxic debris. During the hard labor of examination and preparation, we also acknowledged the brave work of assessing one's environment and its impact on growth. With excitement, we move into the second phase of Spring Stirrings—when A SHIFT Emerges. At the same time, we must not become complacent.

At any time during the process of *SHIFTING Bravely*, the conditions of our soil can and will change. They may become more enriched. Or, they may become contaminated. And, this is true for our environments as well. They may remain safe and secure. Or, they may become highly unhealthy and harmful. With this awareness, we need not cower or cave. Instead, we move ahead with confidence and courage. Even when things are uncomfortable and uncertain, we know how hard we have worked to get here. We know what we need to do. We must return to the process of examining, preparing, and assessing our soil and its surroundings. Our seeds are depending on us. And once again, after we have tended to our soil and cleared the way for our seeds to emerge, we eagerly anticipate entering into the second phase of Spring Stirrings.

When A SHIFT Emerges, we can sense it. We can feel it. In Cynthia Occelli's words, "For a seed to achieve its greatest expression, it must come completely undone." Our roots begin to develop more fully and move deeper into the earth. After the "shell [of the seed] cracks, its insides come out and everything changes" (Occelli). Our stems strengthen, searching for the soil's surface and breaking through. Growth is made evident to the naked eye in the form of a bud or leaf.

During the period of what Occelli describes "becoming completely undone," we are discovering and uncovering new pieces about ourselves. We are exploring who we are and how we want to be. We are entertaining new thoughts and testing out different paths or action steps. We are questioning our past and wondering about our present and future. It is a time of great uncertainty and a time of immense possibility. And although initially we may not see proof of growth, we feel the change within us. It is both humbling and it is empowering.

From the stories of "A SHIFT In My Life" and from clients' stories, there was wide variation in the growing process when A SHIFT Emerges. Much like a diverse garden filled with an assortment of seeds, some SHIFTS emerged rather quickly while others took more time. Still, there were other experiences where a SHIFT started to emerge, was met with a bit of resistance or redirection, but then its budding emergence surprisingly created another SHIFT.

And, SHIFTS emerged largely, but not entirely, from two distinct paths. First, some SHIFTS began emerging from mental processes that involved gaining knowledge and comprehension. These cognitive processes include thinking and talking through, reflecting, praying, meditating, listening, learning, problem-solving, and so on. While spending time processing cognitively, individuals began experiencing SHIFTING beliefs, feelings, thoughts, and attitudes. Over time, as these beliefs, feelings, thoughts, and attitudes became clearer and directive, individuals moved forward making actionable choices or decisions.

Example of a cognitive-based emerging SHIFT:

> A time of reflection (or other cognitive processes) begins the process of SHIFTING our beliefs, feelings, thoughts, and attitudes.
>
> These SHIFTS in our beliefs, feelings, thoughts, and attitudes lead to action steps.
>
> This, in turn, stimulates more reflection (or other cognitive processes).

For others, the second pathway for emergence unfolded slightly differently. Depending upon individual circumstances or unique situations, some individuals began their SHIFTING process by diving into an action plan first. Sometimes this was out of discomfort or desperation. Sometimes, a more natural timeline unfolded, as individuals planned out their course of action. As individuals moved through their actionable steps, a SHIFT in beliefs, feelings, thoughts (or other cognitive processes), and attitudes also began emerging.

Example of an action-based emerging SHIFT:

> Actionable steps begin the process of SHIFTING.
>
> As a result of these actions, SHIFTS begin to emerge in our beliefs, feelings, thoughts (or other cognitive processes), and attitudes.
>
> These dynamic beliefs, feelings, thoughts, and attitudes become stimuli for further action.

Let's take a look at a few examples of action-based emerging SHIFTS from prior stories.

In Chapter One, A SHIFT Lies Dormant, we were introduced to Annika. After years of alcohol addiction where she "managed to destroy her [my] marriage, relationships, trust, and all her [my] self-worth and dignity," Annika entered treatment. Annika heard the calling of her seeds and turned inward, tending to her recovery. When she left treatment, she acquired a job in the field of sobriety while "attending intensive outpatient treatment." It was during this time of processing and understanding of her soil when Annika experienced the beginnings of growth, when A SHIFT Takes Root.

When we pick up with her story, we can feel the excitement in Annika's voice as she describes a domino of changes brought on by her emerging SHIFT. Annika's story illustrates how taking action steps first provided her with time to experience the positive consequences of her actions. This, in turn, shifted her into a cognitive modality of praying, which then supplied fuel for another action step.

> I actually got really good at my job, peddling a liquid vitamin at Costco stores in the Portland, Oregon locations. Things were looking up. My daughter let me move in with her and her husband, if I paid rent (which I did). But this arrangement was on a very strict timeline, given to me by my daughter and my son-in-law.
>
> Well, unfortunately, things were not moving along as fast as I planned with another living arrangement. I was going to rent a room from a friend of mine who was having a house built, but the timing was not working out. I was forced to ask my 'landlord daughter' and her husband for an extension. They declined. I was devastated.
>
> I was embarrassed and ashamed I was in this position. I only needed two more weeks. How could they not help me? I thought… 'This is family?' I withdrew to my room where I lay on my bed (one of my few remaining belongings) and prayed for an answer—a solution.
>
> Then, it dawned on me, a light bulb went on. I thought, 'I don't have to live here anymore! I can move anywhere!' My dream was always to go back home to California. Could this happen? How?
>
> So, I immediately called my boss of the vitamin company and asked her if I could do this same job in California. She said, yes! I then called my sister in CA and told her what I was thinking. She was thrilled!

One of the wonders of Annika's story is witnessing how she spent very little time wallowing in embarrassment and shame. As A SHIFT Emerges, we see how Annika not only remained committed to her recovery program but also experienced success professionally—"I actually got really good at my job."

Annika's path of action produced a sense of self-confidence and self-reliance. Feeling more positive about herself, Annika's mind was open to new considerations and possibilities. Spending time in prayer, her SHIFT then materialized rather quickly—"It dawned on me, a light bulb went on. I thought, 'I don't have to live here anymore! I can move anywhere.'"

And although Annika did not see a clear path ahead, she didn't let it stop her seeds from "coming completely undone." She immediately called her boss to secure employment and reached out to her sister. For Annika, who had lost everything during her years of alcoholism, a developing trust in herself was a testament to her Spring Stirrings and her seasonal process of self-growth.

From the stories of Enrique and Robert, we witness two more examples of seeds that took root in similar ways but began SHIFTING at different paces. First, let's return to Enrique's story from Chapter One, A SHIFT Lies Dormant.

We recall how Enrique was struggling with health issues after pushing himself for twenty-five years in his professional pursuits as a teacher and psychotherapist. His levels of discomfort caused him to turn inward as his health declined and he "went from doctor to specialist to doctor." During the examination and preparation of his soil, Enrique discovered how his life message of "I would rather wear out than rust out" was no longer serving him well.

Although Enrique retired from his teaching career in December 2019, he did not experience his SHIFT's birth until the "COVID pandemic helped slow everything down." Enrique made the decision to cut back on his work hours and began investing into projects less stressful but still meaningful. In slowing down his life, Enrique's seeds continued to crack open and to "come completely undone."

> The shift came with more time, better health, and recognition that I did not need to work so much. My body was responding positively. I FINALLY got the message I was OK financially and wouldn't need to work ever again.

Enrique's story sheds light on two very important aspects of the emerging process. First, Enrique's declining health caused him to make a decision regarding retirement from teaching. There are times where we are required to take action steps even when we are uncertain as to their potential benefit to our growing process. Enrique's reduction in his work hours along with an imposed period of stillness during the pandemic created a more intense period of internal examination. By taking that initial step and trusting in his stillness, Enrique created space for his stem to begin developing and strengthening.

Second, Enrique's process of emergence portrays so importantly how some SHIFTS move at a steady moderate pace—"The shift came with more time, better health, and recognition I did not need to work so much." Enrique's process also demonstrates how one SHIFT impacts another.

Incredibly, Enrique could feel the changes—"My body was responding within." Concurrently, his SHIFT was spreading into his thinking. His growing self-awareness messaged him about what he needed and didn't need—"I FINALLY got the message I was OK financially and wouldn't need to work ever again." Ironically, Enrique's changes in attitude fueled his next action step, permission to retire.

Robert's story is similar to Enrique's in that action steps preceded the emerging SHIFT. However, unlike Enrique's whose SHIFT emerged at a slow steady pace over several months, Robert's rising SHIFT grew over a longer span of time, while intensifying within him.

Returning to Robert's story, we recall how he and his parents owned a large family country club. As a young man, Robert discovered his passion—"By the mid-sixties I was falling in love with education...not schools but learning and teaching." With mutual understanding, Robert and his parents agreed to sell the family business, freeing both parties to live out their dreams. In Robert's words, we witness how his carefully executed plan unfolded over several years, leading up to his "coming completely undone."

> By 1968, the land and the club were sold, my parents were free, and I put all my energies into teaching and education.
>
> Bang! A whole new direction and life opened up for me—a life I had never imagined! Because of this shift, I was able to take all of the skills I had learned growing up and apply them to future challenges..."

Robert's SHIFTING process began with intentional action steps. Although it took several years before his SHIFT actually emerged, it is important to note how Robert's patience and perseverance did not diminish. During the years of problem-solving, organizing, and planning, Robert's seeds were eagerly anticipating their arrival. And when it came time, another action step was taken—"By 1968...I put all my energies into teaching and education." As everything came completely undone, Robert's elation over his long-awaited "coming completely undone" burst through him—"Bang! A whole new direction and life opened up for me."

We can feel the exuberance in Robert's dynamic SHIFT as he begins the process of exploring who he is and how he wants to be! We can sense how his life is about to change, full of immense possibility and growth. Without negating the hard work it took to close out a family business in order to lay the groundwork for his SHIFT, Robert's emergence seems to have come to fruition because of a strong, innate calling within him. It was a calling he could not deny, where well-planned action steps paved the way.

However, there are times after we have cleared our soil and our calling is present, where embarking on actions steps can be grueling. It requires we trust in our growing process and we remain vulnerable in doing so. Returning to Margot's story from Chapter Four, A SHIFT Takes Root, we recall how she has carefully, cautiously, and courageously moved through her seasonal process of self-growth. The cracking open of her shell and the surfacing of her stem were no different.

After being raised in a dysfunctional family, leaving home and entering into an abusive marriage, and then divorcing and living alone, Margot spent years tending to her soil: "After years of adjusting to independence, I was still mostly unhappy and depressed, although some antidepressants had taken the edge off of the depression." Contributing to her unhappiness and depression was the presence of unrelenting shame-filled life messages. As we discussed in A SHIFT Lies Dormant, life messages are our internal dialogue (or messaging) composed from our life experiences and are predominantly influenced by our primary caregivers. They form our personal truths about ourselves. Although Margot struggled while confronting and breaking through them, she persevered and continued to take action steps, although it was painstakingly difficult to do so.

> I consciously made the decision to push myself though events that terrified me, like joining a child protection council, doing volunteer work, and socializing more. I recall crying uncontrollably with fear before I went to these, but I made myself go anyway. That was the start of some life changes.
>
> To do those things, I used what I called the 'boot-strap' method. If I didn't want to do something I knew was good for me, or if I was too afraid to do it, I would pray and ask for the desire to do it. When the desire came, I would pray for the courage to do it. Eventually I always received the desire to try something and to do it even if I was afraid.
>
> Along with the 'boot-strap' method, for the second time in my life I found a caring and effective therapist. She was the support I needed to continue on.
>
> From that point on, the SHIFT in my life really began to change me. I was determined to become emotionally healthy and make a good life for myself, with respect and confidence. The third thing that changed my life, besides the 'boot-strap' method

and working with a therapist, was my determination to be happy despite my circumstances. I changed my attitude and my feelings about my past. I began believing and trusting in my newly unearthed truth, 'I am not what happened to me. I am what I choose to become.'

Margot's story of emergence is powerful on several levels. First, as Margot began taking her action steps, she describes how frightening the process was—"I consciously made the decision to push myself though events that terrified me."

It is important to acknowledge that even when we want to change our direction, it can be very scary. There is nothing comfortable about uncertainty or risk. Margot fought her way through her fears. She did not cave into them.

Second, in preparation for her action steps, Margot leaned into her cognitive process of "boot-strapping"—"I would pray and ask for the desire to do it. When the desire came, I would pray for the courage to do it." This is also important. Margot knew what action she wanted and needed to take, but she also knew she had to mentally prepare herself to take those steps. Not only did she turn to her faith for confirmation, but she also enlisted the support of a caring therapist. She did her own work, but she didn't have to do it alone.

And third, we witness how SHIFTS, that emerge from actions and are enriched through support, fertilize our soil for further growth. As Margot describes, "the SHIFT in my life really began to change me." Margot's seeds began to "come completely undone'' (Occelli) as their emergence reshaped her attitudes and beliefs about her past and her future—"I am not what happened to me. I am what I choose to become." With incredible faith, perseverance, and strength, Margot's shell split open, her roots deepened as her stem surged, and everything changed.

We have been exploring examples of stories where actionable steps began the process of when A SHIFT Emerges. Let's examine a couple of stories where the process of emergence begins within a cognitive-based experience.

Returning to Britt's story in Chapter Four, A SHIFT Takes Root, we recall how Britt viewed herself as a failure. After her mother and her older sister messaged her for years regarding Britt's ineptness and inadequacies, Britt was filled with shame and anxiety. This anxiety eventually led to severe "gut issues" due to Britt's internalization of them as her truths. When we left off with Britt's story, we learned how she worked tirelessly during her time of internal cleansing sorting through her false life messages and forming new truths: "This early messaging was not really about me, even though it affected me deeply. This was about my mother and older sister's need to feel in control and empowered."

As we revisit her story, it is important to note Britt began a deep dive into her cognitive work during A SHIFT Takes Root. We recall her words: "Once I knew what to look for, I could see the pattern in my relationship with my mother and older sister, both past and present. It has taken me many years to acknowledge that inner voice and disempower it."

Witnessing the arrival of her SHIFT, we see once again how Britt relies heavily on a cognitive-based process for confronting falsehoods and for continuing authentic growth.

> I have learned to expect my inner voice [of shame and inadequacy] to begin a conversation. Because I am SHIFTING and no longer embrace these earlier beliefs, I am able to move away from the dis-ease and find inner balance and health.
>
> There is a deceptively simple book, *The Four Agreements* by Don Miguel Ruiz, which has also contributed to my process of SHIFTING. Ruiz talks about the 'mitote', the voices filled with assumptions of others that we come to embrace as truth. They are the voices of family, teachers, spiritual leaders, and our culture. By questioning the 'truth' of these assumptions through testing of our own personal belief system in the world, we are able to find reliable messages which ring true and are authentic. We can learn to let go of the ones that no longer apply.
>
> I have learned to trust my gut as a window into my inner self. And, I act accordingly, trusting my truths.

Britt's story is remarkable. Although the cognitive process of recognizing, identifying, and changing destructive life messages may appear simplistic, it is incredibly hard work. The beliefs and assumptions we hold about ourselves from childhood are deeply rooted within us. However, over time, Britt described how she conditioned herself to become acutely aware of their intrusive presence—"I have learned to expect my inner voice [of shame and inadequacy] to begin a conversation." And, as Britt detailed so importantly, as her roots took hold and her stem stretched towards the soil's surface, she arrested their presence and replaced them with empowering self-truths: "Because I am SHIFTING and no longer embrace these earlier beliefs, I am able to move away from the dis-ease and find inner balance and health."

Although Britt's developing growth is largely cognitive-based, it is important to note as her seeds started to "become undone," she risked taking action steps in order to strengthen her seasonal process of self-growth. This meant becoming completely vulnerable by sharing her new-found truths about herself with others.

At the same time, Britt credits her strength in taking action steps and sharing her truths by leaning into her cognitive growth. From *The Four Agreements* by Don Miguel Ruiz, Britt learned how to test false messages and trust her "truths" which were taking residence within her: "By questioning the 'truth' of these assumptions [voices of family, teachers, spiritual leaders, and our culture] through testing of our own personal belief system in the world, we are able to find reliable messages which ring true and are authentic."

We can imagine how scary it must have been for Brit as her stem pushed through the soil, testing her direction and breaking through the surface. As her new truths formed and were displayed, she boldly discarded the old. We find ourselves rejoicing with Britt as everything changed and she was called to a new way of being—"I have learned to trust my gut as a window into my inner self. And, I act accordingly, trusting my truths."

Early into my work as a therapist, I relied heavily on cognitive-behavioral therapy. This is a process of addressing clients' symptoms or presentations through methodical examination of their thought processes and behaviors and how each is impacting the other. Goals of treatment include challenging unhealthy thought patterns and behaviors and learning strategies for changing them. Although I blended in other approaches or modalities as needed, I found that assisting clients to challenge their beliefs and assumptions about themselves was a critical first step in their journeys of self-growth. As we have witnessed through Britt's story and others from "A SHIFT In My Life," as well as clients' stories, the result of re-scripting life messages enabled them to begin making healthy changes in their lives. In other words, as they began believing in themselves and in their mattering, value, and worth, they began acting upon it by embracing healthier behaviors.

Let's return to Suzanne's story from Chapter Four, A SHIFT Takes Root, and explore her cognitive-based emerging SHIFT, that led to making significant changes in her well-meaning but self-harming behaviors.

From Suzanne's story, we recall how she entered therapy to do some inner personal work, a time of self-exploration. After being in addiction recovery for over ten years, she felt a bit stunted in her growth. After several months working together, Suzanne bravely tended to her soil, unearthing a buried trauma—a horrific public act of personal shaming. As we processed the trauma and its impact on Suzanne, "always wanting to disappear," she was able to release its hold on her. Through Suzanne's careful examining, preparing, and assessing her soil, her seeds were provided a safe clear path for development.

For the next several months in therapy, Suzanne continued to address her beliefs, attitudes, thoughts, and feelings. Empowered by her new truth—"I feel like I am starting to understand who I really am"—she remained open and receptive as we explored additional self-shaming life messages birthed from a childhood of narcissistic parental abuse. Her words reflected her pain but also the role she played in her family.

"I was the one who had to be responsible. With my father drinking and my parents fighting all the time, I felt like I had to be the adult. I tried so hard to make sure I was doing everything right and helping with whatever I could, but it was never enough. I was never enough.

"And then, after the shaming incident in high school, when no one stood up for me, I knew it didn't matter. I was on my own."

Suzanne's story illustrates the importance of spending as much time as possible identifying her past shaming life messages and their impact on her. As her therapist, I knew it was important to allow the process to flow, at a safe comfortable pace.

As we continued our work together, I began asking Suzanne to connect her self-shaming life messages to behaviors she engaged in during her teen and young adult years. Although Suzanne started drinking during high school to self-medicate, she recalled how she began giving of herself, her time, and her resources in most of her relationships. And though these selfless acts initially made her feel a sense of worth and mattering, over time they began to take their toll on her.

During our sessions together, she pensively and painfully described her past.

"As I think back... I would do whatever I could to help someone. I thought doing so was a good thing, and it probably was. But then, I did things that hurt me. I was in really sick relationships where I was treated really badly. Even when I knew I should end them, I stayed. I have a lot of horrible stories and bad memories.

"When I think back, I felt I always had to produce, not just for my family. But for anyone. That way, they would like me. They would accept me. I would be worth something."

Several months passed while Suzanne and I sensitively processed her past, validating her truths and connecting them to present-day thoughts and behaviors. And then, one Saturday afternoon Suzanne entered our session with a combined look of exhilaration and relief. She slid into the big brown leather chair, but had a hard time containing her excitement.

"Holli, you know how we have been talking about how I tried to please everyone when I was growing up? And how I never thought about myself and how it was hurting me? Well, this past week I've been thinking about how I am still doing that!"

Suzanne let out a soft sigh but she remained hopeful.

"I actually made out a list of a few people who I have been bending over backwards to help, to do things for, to take care of, to make excuses for…. you name it! And I realize, it's just like when I was younger. I don't feel better about myself at all. In fact, I feel worse. And resentful. And even worse than that, they don't care. They don't show any appreciation. And, they just keep expecting me to keep doing whatever it is I'm doing!"

And with a giant Cheshire cat grin on her face, she pronounced the following, "I'm done doing this! But I need help. Tell me what to do!"

Suzanne's story illustrates two important points. First, as her seed cracked open and her stem was beginning to emerge, we needed to spend additional time sorting and sifting through additional toxins in her soil. Through our cognitive work together, we did just that. As we unearthed Suzanne's self-shaming beliefs, we then connected them to her past unhealthy behaviors. During this tender process, I remained mindful of helping Suzanne to release any additional self-blame or shame around her choices. Slowly, Suzanne came to understand how during a vulnerable period of time, she chose or engaged in behaviors that served her needs or filled her voids even though many of them were harmful to her. In other words, with little or no support, Suzanne did what she needed to do in order to survive.

Second, Suzanne's rising SHIFT was cognitive-based and carefully unfolded over a period of several months. Ample time was provided for Suzanne to connect past beliefs and assumptions about herself to her past behaviors. Because she was in a place of awareness, she was able to transfer those same connections to present-day thoughts of unworthiness and current self-harming behaviors. Making those powerful cognitive connections provided the stimulation her seeds anxiously awaited. "As her shell cracked, its insides came out and everything changed," (paraphrase, Occelli), we soak in Suzanne's words of promise and purpose—"Holli, I'm done doing this! But I need help. Tell me what to do!" Her stem, her emerging self, was bursting to break through.

From that point forward, Suzanne continued her cognitive work. However, she began taking deliberate actionable steps as she tackled her codependency with full force. As the months progressed, Suzanne implemented strong boundaries around her relationships, even ending some that were toxic. At the same time, she remained aware of her vulnerabilities and did not negate the importance of returning to her soil if called to do so, tending to her roots and her stem.

There is a third process for when A SHIFT Emerges. Before we explore it, we must pause and reflect upon the following concept.

Whether the emergence is cognitive-based or action-based, we see how closely interrelated they are. Our beliefs, feelings, thoughts, and attitudes about ourselves largely determine our actions and behaviors. And the reverse is true. Our actions and behaviors largely determine our beliefs, feelings, thoughts, and attitudes about ourselves. Whichever path of emergence—either cognitive or action-based—is available to us, we must remember it is never too late to enter into Spring Stirrings. Let's review the two conditions necessary for a successful entry into Spring Stirrings.

First, when A SHIFT Takes Root, rather than focusing on things outside of ourselves or placing needs of others above our own, we are called upon to be brave, to turn inward, and tend to our soil.

Second, when A SHIFT Emerges, we are also called to make a critical decision—to choose our "self." No matter how big or small the action step is before us or how significant or insignificant the cognitive challenge may be, we must choose our "self."

It may mean taking an action step like quitting a job or starting a new one, which spurs on our journey of self-growth. It may mean implementing an actionable plan such as entering into a recovery program or leaving a toxic relationship which ignites a desire for further cognitive exploration and understanding of ourselves. It may mean moving away from pain-riddled environments and learning how to implement strong boundaries with unhealthy individuals in order to provide space for cognitive clarity and emotional healing.

On the other hand, from a cognitive perspective, it may be challenging underlying beliefs by embracing a spiritual path in search of insight into a new path or different way of being. It may be seeking emotional support and clarifying feelings before embarking on a new direction. It may mean carving out time for reading, learning, and reflection in order to gain deeper meaning as different avenues of change are explored.

Regardless of how the calling shows up, the pathways into self-growth are endless. They are ours for the choosing.

As we have witnessed through the brave stories of others who have chosen to invest into themselves, when the process of emergence begins to unfold, "The shell cracks, its insides come out, and everything changes" (Occelli). With tremendous uncertainty and endless possibility wrapping their arms around us, each of us will experience a unique seasonal process of self-growth. For some, it will be an action-based emerging SHIFT. Others will embrace a cognitive-based emerging SHIFT.

And still, there are others, who may take a third path of self-growth. Similar to the other two paths, it is one that requires tremendous courage, stamina, and strength. It is one that demands complete vulnerability while simultaneously commanding commitment. The third path of emergence incorporates both the cognitive-based and action-based nourishing elements, but it is uniquely birthed within the therapeutic relationship.

> This path takes place within a therapeutic setting—between client and professional therapist—and it is based on trust, connection, and unconditional positive regard. It is within the safety of the therapeutic relationship and within the shared space of comfort and mutual respect where little SHIFTS show up, connect with other related little SHIFTS, linking together to form larger SHIFTS that in turn deepen roots and clear the way for a rising stem.

The Flower who found her way into my office followed this path of emergence.

Over the first six months of working together, the Flower worked tirelessly and courageously on all phases of her seasonal process of self-growth, especially as we witnessed in Chapter Four, A SHIFT Takes Root. Within the trust of our relationship and the therapeutic process, the Flower bravely examined, prepared, and assessed her soil and its environment. Her years of horrific sexual abuses, trauma, and parental neglect filled her soil with hard black clay. We recall how the Flower slowly and methodically removed the toxic debris from her inner being and how she released the shame that engulfed her. And we remember her courage as she moved from her dangerous neighborhood in order to safeguard herself and her recovery path, greatly diminishing familiar and frightening triggers.

And just when the Flower began to settle into the safety and steadiness of her cleansed soil, we recall how her 'man' came into her life. Returning to the Flower's journey, we witness how her seeds came completely undone and how her companion, a slender silver strong Birch tree, lovingly participated in her transformation.

Moving into our eighth month of working together and growing our therapeutic relationship, the Flower and I connected more empathically on several different levels. First, shortly before calling me and coming into therapy, the Flower shared that she had read one of my books— *Daughters Betrayed By Their Mothers: Moving From Brokenness To Wholeness*. Although we never discussed the book, the Flower began to open up about multiple betrayals around her mother, both past and present. When the Flower spoke of her mother, she wilted in the large brown leather chair across from me. The warm smooth pliable fabric held her fragile stem in place, providing the Flower with a sense of safety. She frequently grabbed the ends of her shawl, pulling it tightly around her like a blanket swaddling a frightened newborn. Listening to her stories of betrayal, I held my eyes with hers. She rarely looked away, only momentarily to dry her tears. I continued to listen intently. The warmth in the room was filled with a thick mixture of compassion, empathy, and connection. As the Flower continued sharing her pain, I held the space between us with unconditional positive regard.

Now and then, I nodded gently and softly repeated, "I'm so sorry. That never should have happened."

The Flower would pause, allowing my words to soak into her being. Uncertain or unsure of what to say, the Flower did not respond. And then during a particularly painful session, she searched my eyes for affirmation and confirmation as she cautiously spoke.

"Holli, no one has ever said those words to me before…The first time you said, 'That never should have happened', I didn't believe it. I felt I deserved what I got. I couldn't take in what you were saying. But now, after hearing it time and time again, I believe you…and I believe that those things that happened with my mom should never have happened."

In that moment of joining together through insight and increased understanding, I could feel a little shift. I gently asked the Flower an important question.

"And, do you believe that today your mom's ongoing betrayals of you should not be happening?"

For the first time in nine months, the Flower's eyes reflected a clarity and a confidence I had not witnessed before. She straightened her stem and held her hands together, without shaking. Another little shift emerged, linking with the first. I saw it in her eyes. She felt it. I did too.

"Yes, I do believe that… for the first time in my life, I do."

Over the next several weeks, the Flower and I continued to process her brokenness around her mother. With each falsehood confronted and dislodged, a newly formed truth replaced it. The Flower began developing a deeper trust in herself and her new truths. Knowing there was more to address and sensing her growing strength, I moved into another related area of trauma and of current pain.

We recall from Chapter Four, A SHIFT Take Root, how the Flower endured horrific sexual attacks and abuses throughout her childhood, developmental years, and into most of her adulthood. Family members and trusted individuals, both female and male, perpetrated the violations and perpetuated them. No one protected her. When the legal system was called upon in defense of her, the Flower was mostly ruled against.

Preparing to move into extremely tender areas of trauma with clients, I am vigilant about assessing levels of trust and connection with each one. It was no different for the Flower. Over the past several months, as our relationship grew, the trust between us deepened. The Flower began sharing more of her personal and creative being with me. She brought in exquisite brightly colored pieces of artwork she had painted, excited to share them with me. She dressed in beautifully hand-stitched and carefully sewn dresses she had crafted together from unusual combinations of fabrics and textures. Her joy in explaining how her creations came to be were mirrored in my expressions of appreciation for her talents and gifts.

And then one day, the Flower began bringing me small samples of her home cooked recipes as well as homegrown pickings from her garden. Although therapists must be mindful of ethical boundaries when accepting gifts from clients, I came to understand that the food was not just a gesture of kindness and generosity. It was an *offering*. It was a symbol representing complete vulnerability. The Flower was placing herself in my hands, hands that provided protection, acceptance, and belonging.

As her protector, I slowly and sensitively approached the violations that led to the Flower's collapse at work, almost ten months previously. Moving through the traumatic timeline of abusive events and their ensuing injustices, I safely held the Flower's pain in our protective space. Maintaining a careful pulse on the Flower, I sensed a minor shift as she felt me receive her pain with care and compassion. Her eyes watered. Mine did too.

When her truths came pouring out, I regarded them with dignity and respect. Their acceptance into our space was welcomed, not just by me but by her spirit grandmother—her ancestral protector. And in the warmth of acceptance—without judgement, fear, or shame—the Flower heard her own voice. It was a voice of strength and courage. I heard it too. Another shift made itself known.

Over the next several weeks, we continued navigating through the additional betrayals from her place of work and their legacy of brokenness. The Flower would often pause and say, "Holli, I can tell you this because I know you understand."

In moments of shared suffering, there is nothing more healing and powerful than to be able to say to a client, "Yes, I do." And when the Flower and I met one another in those shared moments in time, in that sacred space, for the first time in her life, the Flower experienced authentic belonging.

She raised her lovely face and spoke with clarity and confidence. "I am not alone. I am not flawed. Others have experienced pain. Others have healed and learned to love themselves. I can too." A larger shift moved within, her "shell cracked, its insides came out, and everything changed" (paraphrase, Occelli). The Flower's powerful truths filled the room. The Flower felt their presence, honoring their significance. I did too. It was remarkable.

From that moment forward, the Flower's SHIFT continued to surface, strengthening her stem and deepening her roots. Her years of victimization from both domestic and foreign betrayers taught the Flower never to trust the intentions of another being. During our ten months working together, the Flower blossomed in the consistency and continuity of the therapeutic relationship. It was honest, reliable, and transparent. Never missing a session and doubling up on sessions through difficult phases of recovering, the Flower learned she could tether herself to another human being, and not be hurt. Although trusting in a net of support was unfamiliar to the Flower, her beliefs strengthened as its reach widened.

Critical to her net of support was the Flower's psychiatrist. Not only did he monitor the Flower's medications and address additional conditions as they surfaced, but he spent time listening to her, really listening. He and I stayed in contact, consulting on the Flower's progress as well as anticipating and addressing any challenges. Our communications were openly shared with the Flower, demonstrating our mutual concern for her and our commitment to her growth.

Lastly, but as importantly, the Flower's 'man,' became an integral support in her expanding net. Over the five or so months of their relationship, the silvery strong Birch tree had proved to be a nourishing force in her life. Each and every Saturday, he gently escorted the Flower to the main doors of my office. Now and then he would smile and say, "Good mornin'," quickly escaping back to the car.

Settling into our session, the Flower described how the tall slender Birch was finding a home in her heart.

"I feel safe with my 'man.' And, he loves to take care of me...it seems to give him meaning and purpose. I've never had that..." The Flower let out a soft chuckle and added, "He anticipates my needs before I even say anything, but he also knows I need my independence and space."

The Flower continued describing how they had developed a routine together, and how they were blending their lives. And then she spoke of how they mirrored one another, and how she could feel a change growing within.

"Once or twice a week, we just sit and talk. Not for long periods of time, but just enough. It's hard for both of us...we've both come from such broken pasts. My 'man' has been through a lot, just as much as I have. Different stuff...but yet the same.

"When we look into each other's eyes, we see each other's pain. There's an understanding... "

And then she added, "I feel like I've been given a gift... And, for the first time in a very long time, I feel like I am worthy of it. I know I have more work to do, but I feel like I am becoming the person I am meant to be."

As the Flower spoke of her worth and of belonging to herself, I recalled the Flower's tireless work of listening to her calling seeds, paying attention to them, tending to her soil, and trusting in her therapeutic process of when A SHIFT Emerges. Her words, "I feel like I am worthy of it," remained suspended between us for several moments culminating in a larger shift—"I feel like I am becoming the person I am meant to be." Her words were a testament to her seeds being able "to achieve their greatest expression" (Occelli).

Gleaning from the stories from "A SHIFT In My Life" and clients' stories, we have rejoiced with them in their journeys of seeds achieving their greatest expression. Regardless of their paths, each remained tirelessly committed, bravely moving through their unique seasonal process of self-growth. And yet, from what we have learned thus far, we are coming to understand and appreciate how *SHIFTING* is dynamic, not static. As much as we might want to bask in the glow of our self-emergence, it is important to prepare ourselves for the next season, Summer Strong, and what it may bring.

Shortly after our most recent session, the Flower called to let me know her leave from work was coming to an end. Although she had a few weeks to prepare for her return, the Flower was to be placed in her same position, in the same environment as her betrayer and his accomplices. After reassuring the Flower we would work together, supplying her with tools and strategies to equip her for re-entry, I wondered about her levels of resilience and readiness.

Were her stem and roots developed enough to endure the harsh environment?

Was the condition of her soil completely clear of toxic debris, able to absorb and withstand some levels of contagion?

Were the beliefs in her worth and in her becoming strong enough for the resistance coming her way?

I believed and trusted they were. Would she?

Exercises—A SHIFT Emerges

Experiencing increasing movement during Spring Stirrings, we feel excitement and anticipation of emerging growth. Take as much time as needed in responding to the chapter questions.

Understanding how your unique path of emergence unfolds increases your *knowing* of your process. This, in turn, empowers you today as well as in the future. Embrace the wonder as your path unfolds. *Feel* your growth, healing, and transformation take hold.

1. In Chapter Five, we learned how our shifts emerge primarily, but not solely, from two distinct paths. One is a cognitive-based path while the other is an action-based path. We also learned that there is a close relationship between the two and one can blend into the other.

    Study the following two paths. Then describe in detail which path connects more closely with your experience and how your shift is emerging.

    ### A cognitive-based emerging SHIFT

    > A time of reflection (or other cognitive process) begins the process of SHIFTING our beliefs, feelings, thoughts, and attitudes.

    > These SHIFTS in our beliefs, feelings, thoughts, and attitudes lead to action steps.

    > This, in turn, stimulates more reflection (or other cognitive processes).

    ### An action-based emerging SHIFT

    > Actionable steps begin the process of SHIFTING.

    > As a result of these actions, SHIFTS begin to emerge in our beliefs, feelings, thoughts (or other cognitive processes), and attitudes.

    > These dynamic beliefs, feelings, thoughts, and attitudes become stimuli for further action.

2. When A SHIFT Emerges, we also learned there is a third path that incorporates both cognitive-based and action-based

elements, but it is uniquely birthed within the therapeutic setting—between client and professional therapist.

If your shift emerged from this setting or if it currently is emerging within this relationship, describe its emergence and the elements that contributed to it. Consider including the following:

> ➢ Experiencing a sense of belonging, connection, safety, trust, empathy, and vulnerability

> ➢ Sharing a space of authenticity, comfort, mutual respect, and unconditional positive regard

> ➢ Feeling understood and heard

> ➢ Experiencing little SHIFTS, then linking them together with other movements, and over time forming larger SHIFTS

3. If you find yourself still struggling with your emergence taking hold or you continue to feel stuck, Chapter Five reminds us of two very important conditions that must be met with consistency, commitment, and courage.

   Review these two conditions. Then, discuss how each one is contributing to your struggle or of being stuck. Describe what is going on. Then, define what you will commit to in order to change it.

   > ➢ First, when A SHIFT Takes Root, you are called upon to be brave, to turn inward, and tend to your soil. Are you doing this work?

   > ➢ Second, when A SHIFT Emerges, you are also called to make a critical decision—to choose your "self." No matter how big or small the action step is before you or how significant or insignificant the cognitive challenge may be, you must choose your "self." Are you falling back into unhealthy patterns of thinking, behaving, or feeling, or returning to unhealthy relationships? Who or what else is preventing you from choosing you?

4. Whose story in A SHIFT Emerges most closely resembles your path of emergence? Explain why and how it connects with your path.

Season Three:
Summer Strong

6 A SHIFT Faces Recurring Resistance

"All changes, even the most longed for, have their
melancholy..."

Anatole France

Beginning with Winter Stillness and moving through Spring Stirrings, we
have come to appreciate the significance of their seasonal order within the
cycle of growth and of their interdependence. In other words, although an
individual's successful navigation through each phase is a reliable
predictor of a maturing seasonal process of self-growth, there are times
when we may be called upon to return to a prior phase for further exploration and attention. We learned this is especially true for when A SHIFT
Takes Root. Even after we have thoroughly examined, prepared, and
assessed our soil and its surroundings, circumstances can shift and change
at any time altering the healthy condition of our soil, compromising its
essence and integrity. And like purposeful gardeners, we learned how we
must pause, return to our soil and tend to it.

Thus far, throughout a seasonal process of self-growth, we have
witnessed within stories from "A SHIFT In My Life," as well as through
clients' stories, countless occurrences where individuals encountered
internal and external forms of resistance, embraced them, and moved
through them. Understanding "All changes, even the most longed for,
have their melancholy..." (France) allows us to move forward into our
next season Summer Strong with a mindset of courageous openness to
adversity and an ongoing commitment to overcoming it.

As gardeners must do once growth begins to announce itself in various
forms, we do not become complacent in tending to its protection and
promoting its advancement. It is the wise gardener who plans and
prepares for environmental foes such as disease, dangerous insects, wind,
heat, and drought. Thus, regardless of our confidence and courage within

our growing emergence, we too must expect differing forms of opposition, when A SHIFT Faces Recurring Resistance. We must also learn how to manage and move through their presence. In some cases, we may need to consider distancing ourselves from them.

From the stories of "A SHIFT In My Life" and clients' stories, we will explore two sources of resistance: internal and external. Although there is overlap, it is important to differentiate between them and understand how they may interrupt our cycle of self-growth. More importantly, we learn from their stories how confronting challenges and overcoming them strengthens a seasonal process of self-growth. Let's explore a couple examples of internal resistance.

In Britt and Margot's stories from Chapter Five, A SHIFT Emerges, we recall how both worked tirelessly on unearthing and identifying their internal source of resistance—shaming life messages from childhood. More importantly, we remember how each courageously committed to disempowering her life messages by replacing them with messages of self-worth and mattering. We also witnessed their growing understanding of their vulnerabilities and of trusting in themselves.

As Britt's SHIFT emerged, she affirms her growth—"I learned to trust my gut as a window into my inner being." Returning to her story, we see how she is well-prepared to take on any resurgence of internal resistance.

> I know where she [inner self] dwells and when she is in balance. I am more finely attuned to manipulation by others, by those who would steal the power of someone who is vulnerable to enrich themselves.
>
> I have learned to embrace the fear and move through it...

From Britt's words, we glean two important and powerful lessons. First, Britt knows herself very well and trusts herself. Because she is acutely aware of when she is "in balance," she is easily able to detect a threat—"I am finely attuned to manipulation by others." Because she is confident in her self-awareness and self-growth, Britt does not default to other forms of internal resistance such as denial, minimization, or rationalization. She is well-grounded in her truths as she takes on these tests.

Second, Britt understands her feelings and accepts them as a part of her being. She neither diminishes them nor cowers to them—"I have learned to embrace the fear and move through it." What courage Britt demonstrates as she leans into the fear. Securing herself in her truth that fear no longer controls her, she bravely manages it.

And in a similar fashion within Margot's story, we witnessed how she identified her debilitating shaming life messages from childhood—"...all my mother had to give me was my birth...and I could never do anything right." As Margot's SHIFT emerged, she began replacing them with her new truth—"I am not what happened to me. I am what I choose to become." In order to safeguard against falling back into toxic patterns of thinking and regressing into extreme feelings of social anxiety, Margot describes her process for confronting her internal forms of resistance as she continues to grow and flourish.

> Over the years, I have immersed myself in reading and learning about healthy ways of becoming emotionally stronger. I have continued with my therapy, along with leaning more into practices of praying and meditating.
>
> Although this may sound strange, I have spent time quietly observing others to learn social skills. By learning to really listen to others, it has calmed my anxiety and helped me to interact more naturally. I am still learning.
>
> I know it is my job to continue lifting myself up.

Margot's story portrays so beautifully and authentically how she has not become complacent in her growth. She continues to fortify herself with protective measures such as "reading, learning, praying, and meditating." And in her ongoing struggle with social anxiety, she turns to a healthy internal source of support—"quietly observing others... and learning to really listen." With self-compassion, Margot explains how these subtle tools have calmed her anxiety and helped her to interact more naturally.

Remarkably, just as Britt does, Margot enthusiastically and whole-heartedly embraces her role in advocating for her self-growth—"I know it is my job to continue lifting myself up."

Destructive life messages are a formidable source of internal resistance. However, there are many others that show up prior to and during the emerging process and pose a threat to our self-growth. A few of the most common include doubting ourselves, denying our needs, and diminishing our truths. Let's return to a client's story from Chapter Two, A SHIFT Is Awakened, and learn how one individual confronted them and moved through them.

Briefly, we were introduced to Phillip in Chapter Two. We recall he is a forty-nine-year-old male who is unhappy in his marriage. During his time in therapy, Phillip has worked extremely hard on his codependency.

Instead of focusing all his energies on taking care of everyone and everything and losing himself in the process, Phillip is learning to take care of his needs. During the past several months, Phillip has paid attention to his seeds' calling, prepared his soil, and experienced a sizable shift in his seasonal process of self-growth. Phillip remains a compassionate and caring person; however, he no longer is rescuing family members or over-investing into them to the point where he is angry and resentful. Although it has been Phillip's desire to heal himself and to save his marriage, recently his wife moved out and filed for divorce.

As we continue working together, Phillip is making significant progress. However, he frequently regresses into patterns of unhealthy thinking, internal forces working against his growth.

"Maybe I should have tried harder. Maybe I wasn't a good provider or a good father...I really worked hard at making sure my kids and wife got their needs met.

"I wonder if my wife is right, it's all my fault. I should have been more fun, not so serious all the time. It's just that if I didn't get things done, nothing would get done!"

Phillip's words are reflective of a recurring form of internal resistance, a belief that he alone is responsible for taking care of everyone's needs and that he has failed to do so. They reveal his self-doubt and denial of his needs. Because of Phillip's codependent nature, he is accustomed to devaluing himself. Each time Phillip comes face to face with these negative thoughts of "over-responsibility" and entertains their legitimacy, he sabotages his growth. On the contrary, each time Phillip confronts these cognitive distortions, deconstructs their false nature, and reconstructs them with truth-based experiences, he strengthens his development.

Recently, Phillip shared the following in our therapy session.

"It's taken me a while but I'm seeing how I felt responsible for my wife's complaints and my kids' problems. I thought I needed to fix everything and everyone.

"I do know I made mistakes, and I also now understand they made them as well. It feels so good not to attach their choices or behaviors to my worth or value as a father or former husband.

"I'm taking it day by day. But each time that negative self-talk pops into my head, I stop it and replace it with something positive. It's hard! And, it works!"

Phillip's story reveals two very important takeaways. First, just because we have experienced a significant SHIFT doesn't mean that old patterns of thinking, behaving, and feeling are going to immediately disappear or never show up again. They have been part of our way of being for a long time. We don't need to beat ourselves up. We need to be patient with ourselves and persevere, just as Phillip is doing—"I'm taking it day by day. But each time that negative self-talk pops into my head, I stop it and replace it with something positive."

Second, as we continue growing, it is important to acknowledge our weaknesses or past unhealthy behaviors with honesty. In Phillip's words, "I do know I made mistakes." At the same time, it is critical not to stay there. In advancing our growth, we need to remain focused on our process and the benefits of it. As Phillip states, "It feels so good not to attach their choices or behaviors to my worth or value as a father or former husband."

As we have witnessed in Phillip's story, internal forms of resistance emanate from our core being—who we have been for a very long time—require us to be mindful of their recurring presence and tend to them in a timely manner. Interestingly, from one of the stories in "A SHIFT In My Life," a similar internal form of recurring resistance not only tested the individual throughout her seasonal process of self-growth, but it actually served as a catalyst for another SHIFT.

Returning to Naomi's story in Chapter Two, A SHIFT Is Awakened, we recall how she entered into a period of personal exploration and discovery. After spending thirty years dedicating herself to her roles as a loving wife and mother of three and after ending a twenty-year job in the legal field, Naomi was "looking forward to starting a path of self-growth, spiritual growth, and rediscovering who she really was and what her purpose was."

After her seeds were awakened and she listened to their call, Naomi began her journey of self-exploration. Unfortunately, her plans were derailed when her older daughter entered into a period of self-destructive drug addiction. Naomi, much like Phillip, fell back into her familiar role as caregiver, desperately trying to rescue her daughter. As her daughter continued to decline, Naomi turned inward and began tending to her soil—"I had to save me"—even as her codependency remained a relentless foe.

Picking up with her story, as Naomi's SHIFT strengthens and surfaces, we witness how she struggles with recurring patterns of thinking and behaving, denying her own needs in order to meet her daughter's. And yet, as her story unfolds, we are astounded by her honesty, courage, and tenacity as she faces additional internal resistance shifting her into a more powerful phase of transformation.

In September 2008, my daughter finally flew back home. I felt so relieved until I saw her. She had lost a significant amount of weight, and her appearance supported her drug use. It was so difficult to accept as our daughter had been the perfect child, in every way. She excelled in school, sports, and was never a rebellious child. All I knew was my daughter was the shell of who she was.

My husband and I were told by our therapist that we had to stop enabling our daughter with money and that I had to let her go...and I could not save her. I felt like I was drowning and being sucked into a whirlpool down the drain. Once again, I was reminded that this was not about my daughter. It was about me.

I continued with therapy sessions, which were helpful. During this time, another SHIFT occurred when I realized I had deep rooted issues beginning in early childhood. Painful recollections surfaced of emotional abuse, codependency, and trying to be perfect in the eyes of my mother who suffered from Borderline Personality Disorder. These memories were overwhelming.

Because of that SHIFT, I answered a nudge which had been laid on my heart. I traveled to Sedona, Arizona, where I took part in a retreat, embarking on a personal path to my healing. After the intensive groundwork I completed in Sedona, it took several months for me to finally see the light.

The despair and angst throughout my journey of self-growth had to happen to me. Because of them, I was able to uncover the betrayals from an unloving mother, the struggle to survive, and the uncovering of masks I had placed in order to survive.

Naomi's story is incredibly compelling on several levels. First, it portrays the relentless nature of internal resistance—"I felt like I was drowning and being sucked into a whirlpool down the drain," and of Naomi's commitment to overcoming it. Reaching out for support from her therapist who addressed Naomi's rescuing of her daughter, Naomi courageously redirected her energies towards her growth—"Once again, I was reminded that this was not about my daughter. It was about me."

Second, Naomi did not deny, minimize, or rationalize her codependent nature and her struggle with it. In fact, she remained open to further self-exploration of it—"I continued with therapy sessions, which were helpful." What is remarkable is that within her season of emergence, Naomi simultaneously continued tending to her soil and unearthing particles of past pain: "During this time, another SHIFT occurred when I realized I had deep rooted issues beginning in early childhood. Painful recollections surfaced of emotional abuse, codependency, and trying to be perfect in the eyes of my mother…These memories were overwhelming."

Although Naomi states, "During this time another SHIFT occurred," I believe her words reveal a third and a uniquely unanticipated gift of growth within her process. As Naomi courageously worked through her internal resistance of codependency around her daughter, she unknowingly awakened a different but related dormant seed and heard its calling—"I realized I had deep rooted issues beginning in childhood." Naomi did not cower or cave. She paid attention to this seed—"I answered a nudge which had been laid on my heart"—and she tended to it—"I traveled to Sedona, Arizona where I took part in a retreat, embarking on a personal path to my healing."

It is also critical to point out how Naomi's process of self-growth has been riddled with internal resistance the entire way. It has not hindered her growth. It has expanded it. It has strengthened its legitimacy. In her words, "The despair and angst throughout my journey of self-growth had to happen to me. Because of them, I was able to uncover the betrayals from an unloving mother, the struggle to survive, and the uncovering of masks I had placed in order to survive."

I cannot think of a better testament to the perseverance and resilience during a seasonal process of self-growth. At any time, Naomi could have given up and given in. She could have relapsed into her former unhealthy way of being. Instead, like a steadfast gardener, Naomi did not abandon her "self" when forces worked against her, resisting her growth. She embraced them, moved through them, and emerged more strongly than before.

With increased awareness, we are coming to understand how different forms of internal resistance are a natural occurrence within our unique journeys. We must not be ashamed or embarrassed by their presence or intrusion into our process. We must acknowledge them and address them, one at a time, as our transformation continues to form and flourish. Let's explore one more example of internal resistance, one that is unexpected and unsettling.

Thus far, it has been quite a growing journey through Winter Stillness and Spring Stirrings. And as A SHIFT Emerges, we broke through our soil and burst onto the landscape.

And unexpectedly, whether we are experiencing a strong and sizable emergence or a more subtle and steady one, there is often an eerily quiet and extremely confusing form of internal resistance taking residence within our being—a state of unease. It is within this state of uneasiness, we find ourselves being newly vulnerable.

Yes, we are excited. But we are also anxious. Yes, we are confident. And, we are uncertain. Yes, we feel competent, but we still know there is risk ahead. We recognize we are changed and yet we are still changing. We wonder if it is real and if it is sustainable. Everything we have been working for or towards is coming to fruition. But now, we are not certain what to do next or if we are really equipped to do it at all.

This vulnerability is normal. Whether we are entering into a new career, embracing a new phase of recovering, engaging in new relationships, or embarking on new adventures, discoveries, or opportunities, there will be a mixture of accomplishment and trepidation. In our new vulnerability, one minute we will doubt ourselves and everything we are doing. The next moment, we will know we are precisely where we are supposed to be.

During this period of unease, and any recurring episodes that follow, we must resume the role of a gardener. We acknowledge the unease, we pay attention to it, and if need be, we tend to it. And as we did when we moved through the prior phases in our cycle of growth, we acknowledge the importance of commitment and we take confidence in the growth we've achieved. Most importantly, like a patient gardener we move forward with the understanding it takes time for new growth to establish itself. Like a wise gardener, we remain open to what the emerging process is teaching us.

Let's continue to increase our understanding and strengthen our arrival as we move through Summer Strong.

Although A SHIFT Faces Recurring Resistance from internal sources, external forms of resistance are equally pervasive. As with internal examples, some may appear more mildly and have a shorter life span while others may present more severely and are longer lasting. Regardless of how external sources of resistance show up in our process of self-growth, being aware of them and learning how to navigate through them strengthens our emerging "new self."

From "A SHIFT In My Life," we will look at how external resistance played out in the life of one committed individual.

From Jazmine's story from Chapter Four, A SHIFT Takes Root, we remember how Jazmine paid attention to the calling of her seeds, turning her life around by leaving an abusive relationship and quitting her job as a dominatrix. With a desire to honor her ancestors' service in the military, Jazmine's transformation began as she enlisted into the U.S.

Army. Because Jazmine was placed in the "delayed entry program," she was afforded additional time tending to her soil and clearing it for growth.

Returning to Jazmine's process of emergence, we witness how as her growth strengthens, she is simultaneously working through sensitive and consequential external forces of resistance.

> In Basic Training, I was able to build up my self-confidence by proving to myself I was able to achieve and to be mentally and physically strong enough to do all that was required of me. I was even made squad leader.
>
> I also learned to like myself a little. After all, my Squad and Drill Instructor seemed to like me, and dare I say, respect me.
>
> Of course, I still had many secrets that were not safe to share with them [military]. I was gay, I had worked in a massage parlor, and been involved with drugs….and so on. However, I found ways to navigate the questions that could [at that time] get me kicked out of the service.
>
> I took to the discipline and discovered healing from my emotional pain. Somehow, I used my rage for energy to help me with the double-time marches, obstacle courses, and rifle range qualifications.
>
> Although I was not able to serve in the Vietnam War, due to the delayed entry, I still greatly benefited from all that came from serving in the military.

From Jazmine's story, we glean two important insights into external resistance. First, Jazmine's prior life was filled with numerous external forms of recurring resistance such as abuse, addiction, and illegal activity. By completely changing environments, she freed herself from them and began fully embracing her growing process: "I was able to build up my self-confidence by proving to myself I was able to achieve and to be mentally and physically strong enough to do all that was required of me." Although it is difficult to do so, sometimes we must remove ourselves from environments that run contrary to our self-growth.

Second, just as Jazmine was finding and healing her "self," she could not disclose her sexual orientation—"I still had many secrets that were not safe to share with them [military]. I was gay…"—Jazmine was not free to be her "true self." Because of the laws in place at that time, Jazmine knew the risks of confronting this external force of resistance and chose to conform through silence. In spite of the pain this must have caused Jazmine, she benefited from the positives within the structure of the military—"I took to the discipline and discovered healing from my emotional pain."

Jazmine did not compromise her "self" in her choices. She knew what she was doing and why. For Jazmine, it was a matter of temporarily suspending her truth in order to sustain and strengthen her process of emergence.

When we come up against formidable external forces of resistance embedded within social, cultural, organizational, institutional norms or in any system where there is a power differential with potential severe consequences at stake, we each must decide what is best for us, our integrity, and our process of self-growth. As we strive to advance our growth, we must be able to live with our choices and we must respect ourselves in the process.

Throughout the stories from "A SHIFT In My Life," there was very little reference given to a common form of recurring external resistance—financial constraints. Annika's story in Chapter Five, A SHIFT Emerges, discussed it briefly. After embracing her recovering from alcohol addiction and securing an exciting job, we recall how Annika wanted to move from Oregon to California to pursue her career and start a new life. However, she did not have the funds to do so. In her story, Annika reached out for help. A loving sister who lived in California found a way to assist Annika in her move.

Although this was the only financial hardship mentioned within the SHIFT stories, it has been my experience that countless individuals face this form of external recurring barrier. Not only in my personal life but in my professional careers as a teacher and then a therapist, I have witnessed varying degrees of struggle and severity. While some of us face financial hardship, many others suffer from generational poverty and other forms of economic oppression. Some of us have sources of support and assistance. Many do not. However, it is my belief that facing and tackling financial hardship can serve as a motivating force in a seasonal process of self-growth. More importantly, challenging and overcoming any kind of adversity, financial or otherwise, contributes to the legitimacy and longevity of our emerging self.

As we have learned, external forms of resistance show up in social norms, regulations, rules, and laws often posing a significant challenge to our process of self-growth. At the same time, one of most difficult faces of recurring external resistance shows up in our lives on a more personal level—our relationships with family and friends.

Over the years as a therapist, I have had the privilege of witnessing the transformation of countless individuals. As they are growing, shifting, and changing, they frequently come up against unwanted and unexpected foes—with their families, friends, and others who preferred the old "self." This can be extremely difficult to confront and move through, as it often means creating additional shifts in our relationships. However, it can be done.

Let's return to Suzanne's story in Chapter Five, A SHIFT Emerges. We remember how Suzanne has worked tirelessly on her seasonal process of self-growth. After being in recovery for ten years from alcohol addiction, Suzanne entered therapy. She listened to the calling of her seeds, bravely unearthing a childhood trauma, and she tended to the healing of her soil. As her shift began surfacing, Suzanne identified how her codependent behaviors, birthed during her childhood, were playing out in her adult relationships. Exhausted and depleted from overinvesting into friend-ships, both personally and professionally, as well as with several family members, Suzanne announced in a therapy session, "I am done doing this! Tell me what to do!"

As we continued working together, Suzanne began implementing boundaries around her relationships. This was really hard work for her, especially as she was met with anger and judgment from others. There were numerous occasions when Suzanne slipped back into her codependent role, but time and time again she picked herself up and kept going. She became more aware of her areas of weakness and continued to revisit and shore up her boundaries. During one session, Suzanne revealed the following.

"Holli, sometimes I feel so guilty when I say no to someone. And then family or some of my friends will get mad at me because I'm not doing all the stuff I did for them before.

"I'm using my self-care statements like what we talked about. And, I practice ahead of time so I won't chicken out. I'll say things like 'I know I helped you before, but I need to do what is best for me.' Or, 'I'm not able to help you. You'll have to ask someone else.' But they just look at me with disapproval and sometimes say really hurtful things. If that happens, I just walk away or end the conversation."

Suzanne hesitated and added, "It hurts for a while, but I just give myself some time to move through it. I'm understanding that because I am changing doesn't mean they are. And what is important is I feel so much better about myself."

Suzanne's words reveal two important takeaways. First, when we are faced with resistance from loved ones or from others whom we care about, like Suzanne we can expect to experience discomfort, such as "I feel so guilty" or "It hurts for a while." Knowing ahead of time that we are most likely going to meet such resistance, allows us to prepare for it and to implement self-care measures. There are times when we may need to reduce contact or minimize time spent with folks who continue not to respect our new "self." Over time Suzanne discovered there were a few individuals whose attitudes and behaviors toward her became intolerable. As she became stronger in her emergence and protective of her growth, Suzanne chose to end those relationships.

Second, something magical happens when we challenge our resistance and stay committed to our process. As Suzanne expressed, "And what is important is I feel so much better about myself." When we begin to experience the internalization and continuance of self-growth, when we begin to feel differently, our new "self" basks in the strength of Summer Strong.

Although we have explored a number of faces of internal and external recurring resistance, there may be others. We have come to accept, "All changes, even the most longed for, have their melancholy..." (France). We have come to understand how any threat to our arising "self" can either weaken us or strengthen us. It depends on our response to it.

The Flower's journey was no different.

The Flower found her way through the awakening and calling of her seeds. Bravely, she turned inward and paid attention to them. She spent months tending to her soil's conditions, courageously unearthing mounds of toxic debris and cleansing them from her. And then after ten long months, when A SHIFT Emerges, we witnessed how the Flower began to grow and strengthen as she made herself completely vulnerable, trusting in our therapeutic relationship. Month after month, the Flower fought through formidable forces of internal resistance such as shame, guilt, and self-blame. She never wavered in her commitment and never ceased trusting our process. Slowly and one at a time, insights into her being led to increased understanding of her trauma and its impact on her. Little shifts emerged, connecting with others to form larger ones.

We felt her emergence intensify as she leaned on her psychiatrist for medical support and trusted in his expertise. And, we saw how the Flower began to flourish when her "man" came into her life, proving to be a safe companion and a soulmate who shared in her suffering. We learned how the tall slender Birch found meaning in serving the Flower, but who also respected her independence. As the different pieces of growth blended together, the Flower's blossoming spoke its truth, "I am becoming the person I was meant to be."

In returning to her story, we recall just when the Flower was enjoying her new "self," an external form of resistance presented itself. The Flower's leave from work was coming to an end. She was expected to return to her prior work place, the same environment of harassment where she collapsed almost a year ago.

Over the next several weeks, the Flower doubled up on her sessions. We reviewed all the triggers she had dealt with before and anticipated as many as we could think of. Cognitive-behavioral exercises for managing triggers were revisited and practiced. New ones were added. We role-played, rehearsing conversations with toxic individuals and planning responses as well as preparing respectful exit plans.

As her return date approached, the Flower was ready. Her words spoke volumes.

"Holli, I'm a different person than I was before. I am no longer afraid of them, especially the betrayer. Although they are above me in title and position, they no longer hold power over me."

The weekend before her start date, the Flower received a phone call from her manager. The Flower was to report to a different office at a different location.

Over the next several weeks, the Flower worked very hard in her new position. Most of her duties and responsibilities were foreign to her. The learning curve was extremely high and the Flower thought the management might be looking for a way to dismiss her. She became somewhat fearful. In therapy, we addressed those internal recurring forces of resistance—mind-reading the motives of others.

The Flower identified them and moved through them.

"I know I always do that. I think the worst...I never trust anyone. I think they are out to get me.

"I'm doing what you said. I'm remembering there is no proof of this. I'm making it up in my head. In fact, my new supervisor said I was catching on really well. It's just me...that old self playing those old tapes."

The Flower continued working, learning the ropes of her new role. One day, she received a call from her prior supervisor. The Flower was to return and pick up her belongings which had been boxed up for her. Once again, we prepared for this visit. It did not take much. The Flower's roots, stem, and pedals were growing stronger every day.

After picking up her possessions, the Flower reported on her experience.

"I never thought I would say this but I'm grateful I had to return there. When I collapsed and was placed on leave, I was so ashamed of what happened to me. But now, I had the opportunity to walk in there, pick up my things, and not hide my face. Even with the betrayer and several of his accomplices in the reception area, I held my head high and smiled as I retrieved my belongings.

"When I left this time, I did so with self-respect."

And then the Flower added, "I definitely am becoming the person I am meant to be."

The Flower's story portrays so beautifully two important lessons. First, when we are met with any form of external resistance we choose to confront, it is vital to conduct a brutally honest inventory of our levels of healing and of potential harm in order to prepare adequately. In the Flower's case, she was in a strong place of growth; however, returning to an environment highly charged with triggers placed her at risk for re-injury. With a series of tools at her disposal, the Flower not only navigated toxic territory successfully, but she empowered herself in the process—"I never thought I would say this but I'm grateful I had to return there."

Second, when we choose to face any external form of resistance with the goal of moving through it, we must adopt a singular mindset. This is about us, not them. Thus, if we choose to challenge the resistance, not only must we prepare but we must also be clear on our motives. If we hope that we will change minds or convince others of our worth or value, we are going to be severely disappointed and most likely damaged by the experience. If, like the Flower, we move forward with the sole objective of honoring our "selves," we advance our growth and we protect the integrity of our work. And like a purposeful gardener, if we keep our focus on our growth, we will reap the rewards in doing so. The Flower's words illustrate this beautifully: "Even with the betrayer and several of his accomplices in the reception area, I held my head high and smiled as I retrieved my belongings. When I left this time, I did so with self-respect."

After moving through the external resistance from her prior place of work, the Flower expressed an interest in confronting a more tender, complex source. During periods of her adult life, the Flower maintained a distanced and detached relationship with several family members, including her mother. As her shift continued to surface, the Flower became more intolerant of being ridiculed and demeaned by them. In addition, the Flower's communication with several of them continued to affect her growth adversely.

During one session, the Flower spoke softly but with conviction.

"Holli, whenever I have those night terrors, as you call them, I realize I have recently had a conversation with my mother or with another family member who is still so cruel to me. When I have those horrific dreams, it sets me back for a day or two. It sort of haunts me...I just don't feel like myself.

"Although we've discussed this before, I'm ready to set strong boundaries around my contact with them. It's really hard...and sad...but I know what I need to do."

The Flower's story, once again, reveals another important insight into our emerging process. As we continue to grow, we may find we are more tolerant of some things and less tolerant of others.

This is a significant sign of increased awareness into our process and what is needed to maintain its integrity. And like a gardener who carefully monitors the impact of environmental elements on growth and makes calculated adjustments, we too must assess what nourishes us and what does not. And then, we make changes in order to promote our growth just like the Flower—"I'm ready to set strong boundaries around my contact with them. It's really hard...and sad...but I know what I need to do."

Over the next several months, the Flower continued to flourish. Additional challenges surfaced at work and she tackled them and moved through them. She set strong boundaries with family members and began experiencing an internal release from their haunting of her. Because of her growing strength and confidence, we agreed to lessen our sessions to once a month. Although there was a sadness on my part as well as hers, we both knew she was ready.

And then, one Saturday morning as the Flower approached my office, I noticed she was alone. The tall slender Birch who faithfully escorted her to my door was not with her. We greeted one another and settled into our conversation. As the Flower began to share a very personal internal form of resistance, she wept.

"I'm not sure exactly where to start or if I am able to explain...but things are not good between me and my 'man'."

I listened and waited. As she always did, the Flower spoke with intention and purpose.

"I think things started to change when I got stronger. Although I love how my 'man' serves me and takes care of me, I wanted to do things for myself. And when I've told him, he just shuts down and says I don't need him anymore.

"And then when I went back to work, he felt even more alone and isolated with nothing to do. Even though he takes care of all the household stuff and has dinner ready for me every night, he doesn't feel like he is important to me.

"I don't know what else to do or say."

For the next several minutes, we talked about the Flower's powerful emerging self, how she had changed since meeting her 'man', and how this was a natural outgrowth of her emergence. When one partner shifts and the other does not, it causes friction in the relationship. It takes time and honesty to navigate through the turbulence. Because the Flower and her man continued to communicate well, we discussed ways to talk about their changing roles while honoring each one's position, and how they could take care of their own needs while still remaining sensitive to meeting each other's.

The Flower was receptive to our discussion and yet I felt there was more. I sat quietly and waited for her. She lowered her face, as more tears fell.

"I am a little afraid...My 'man' has started drinking again. When we first met, I told him it was not okay with me...and he stopped. But now, he is drinking more and more."

She raised her face and looked into my eyes. I saw her anguish and her fear.

"I know he is hurting... And I know it's not me. It's all his past abuse... years and years of horrific childhood abuse. I think as long as he could take care of me, it gave him a purpose. But now, he is adrift... numbing his pain."

The Flower's stem straightened and her growth filled the room. A new "self" spoke her truth.

"I told him, God brought me a 'gift', not a drunk. You need to decide which one you want to be."

Watching the Flower as she returned to her car, I reflected on our sixteenth month journey together. I didn't doubt her growth or her ongoing commitment to it. I didn't think for a moment she would trade in her new "self" for the sake of another. And still, I knew of her loneliness, of her longing for a life partner, and of her deep love for a tall, gentle silver Birch.

During this season of Summer Strong, I wondered what changes lie ahead for the Flower.

Even though the Flower longed for this relationship, would she face more melancholy?

And if there were recurring forces of resistance, might the Flower flounder, even as she fought to overcome them?

Or, as the Flower fully emerged to become one with her SHIFT, would she blossom in spite of them?

Exercises—A SHIFT Faces Recurring Resistance

In the beginning phase of Summer Strong, we are reminded how forms of resistance can show up all throughout the growing process. Especially when our shift is emerging, we must remain vigilant about acknowledging and confronting them, moving through them, and in some cases, managing them.

As always, take your time. Move at your own pace. Remember, by knowing your areas of vulnerability, you can prepare and plan for their presence. You do not cower or cave. You continue to travel your path through discomfort, courageously. Your growth, healing, and transformation are strengthened because of it.

1. Review the two areas of recurring resistance and examples within each. Next, describe which examples of resistance you are confronting or barriers you are facing. More importantly, define the practices you are incorporating as you commit to addressing them. If you have experienced other forms of resistance, include them.

Internal forms of recurring resistance

➤ Life messages of shame, guilt, self-blame; a lack of worth, value, mattering, or being enough

➤ Negative thoughts such as doubting yourself, denying your needs, or diminishing your truths

➤ Cognitive distortions such as over-responsibility (It's always my fault) or mind-reading (I know they think I am worthless)

➤ Codependency – investing into someone or something else at the expense of your own wellbeing

➤ Beating yourself up for relapsing or falling back into prior unhealthy behaviors, thought, feelings, attitudes, or relationships

➤ Not allowing yourself time to be patient and to be still

➤ Not reaching out for support, guidance, or counseling when needed

➢ Denying, minimizing, or rationalizing unhealthy behaviors and choices

➢ Not being honest with yourself

➢ Other internal forms of recurring resistance

External forms of recurring resistance

➢ Family, friends, cohorts, peers, colleagues—anyone who prefers your "old self" and resists your "new self"

➢ Unhealthy relationships, both personal and professional

➢ Abusive or traumatic environments

➢ Environments of addiction or other adverse conditions

➢ Environments where there is a power differential with potentially discriminatory or predatory practices

➢ Financial hardship, generational poverty, or other forms of economic oppression

➢ Other external forms of recurring resistance

2. In A SHIFT Faces Recurring Resistance, what strategies are you learning that will help in confronting and managing internal and external forms of recurring resistance? Explain in detail.

3. In A SHIFT Faces Recurring Resistance, we discovered that although most of us are excited and enthusiastic as we feel our shift emerging, we simultaneously are experiencing an eerily quiet and extremely confusing form of internal resistance—a state of unease. In this state of unease, we might be feeling a mixture of confidence and doubt, accomplishment and trepidation, competence and vulnerability.

As you are reflecting on your growth thus far and where it has taken you, describe your mixture of feelings. Then, respond to these questions.

❖ What is surprising to you?

❖ What is scary?

❖ What is affirming or validating?

❖ What are you learning?

4. In A SHIFT Faces Recurring Resistance, whose story do you find
    most compelling? Explain why.

7   **A SHIFT Is Sustained**

"I affirm I am rooted in truth and my truth is allowed
to shift and transform."

Unknown

Eight months ago, my adult daughter embraced a pastime carried down through the generational genes of her maternal grandfather—becoming a gardener. During the quiet of Winter Stillness, she carefully planned out the arrangement of her planter boxes and meticulously plotted out diagrams designating the placement of an assortment of seeds that would inhabit them. Much attention was given to the strategic positioning of selective companion plants so as to ensure a natural process of protection against threats or pests.

In anticipation of Spring Stirrings, the thoughtful gardener researched differing types of soil. Selecting the best composition for her desired outcomes, she methodically prepared each box for planting. Seeds for an assortment of tomatoes, squash, kale, peppers, and a variety of herbs/spices found their homes within the rich warm, damp soil. Small colorful, scentful flowers and plants dotted the dark soil, serving as guardians over them. The warmth of Spring nourished the seeds, as roots began to grow and stems broke out of their shells. Every morning, without fail, the mindful gardener lovingly tended to her garden beds, monitoring their levels of water and of light and checking for any kind of disturbance. As Spring Stirrings came to a close, the purposeful gardener witnessed the beginnings of growth, eagerly awaiting their full emergence.

Summer Strong brought warmth needed for ongoing development. Wire cylinder structures were constructed to provide support for tomato plants running wild. Stakes were erected with nets strung between them to protect more fragile plants from the intense heat and winds. The nurtured plots of produce not only emerged, they surged. The gardener and her family began to partake in the gifts of growth as each day brought a cornucopia of bounty.

And then, in the beauty of ever-present growth, rampant wildfires roared through the mountainous areas of Northern California. Intense heat, wind, and ash filled the air and covered the landscape for miles and miles. With the threat of fire destruction nearing their property, the young gardener and her family evacuated to safety. Ten long days passed before a return home was permitted. Grateful that her town and her home were spared, the anxious gardener expected to see her beloved beds holding the skeletons of her precious plants, unable to survive amidst extreme forces of external resistance.

But Summer Strong was not willing to succumb to such a fate. To her astonishment, the garden inhabitants not only survived, they thrived. Without a drip system in place, there was simply no explanation, except one. Tethered to their organic strength nurtured and fostered deeply within, the resilient bodies of growth sustained themselves. The bountiful array of vegetables huddled beneath the leafy canopies was a testament to it.

Moving into the fullness of Summer Strong, we too can claim that strength. One of the beautiful gifts of *SHIFTING Bravely* is *knowing* how our growth is capable of sustaining us. Our *knowing* is evidenced by a clear differentiation between our truths about ourselves and our ways of being prior to our SHIFT in comparison to during and after our SHIFT. These new truths show up in our attitudes, beliefs, and feelings as well as in our actions, behaviors, and choices.

As we move into and through Summer Strong, it is important to acknowledge and affirm the embodiments of our strength and to recognize the evidence of our growth. In doing so, not only do we validate our seasonal process of self-growth but we also empower ourselves *knowing* A SHIFT Is Sustained.

In my work as a therapist and in my personal journey, I am drawn to books, passages, and poems that speak to growth and empowerment. In preparation for writing Chapter 7, I stumbled across a poem outlining the hallmarks of when A SHIFT Is Sustained. Although there may be other signs of our SHIFT's solidification within our being, most of us will experience some or all of the following:

> "As you are shifting, you will begin to realize you are not the same person you used to be.
> The things you used to tolerate have become intolerable.

When you once remained quiet, you are now speaking your truth.

Where you once battled and argued, you are now choosing to remain silent.

You are beginning to understand the value of your voice and there are some situations which no longer deserve your time, energy, and focus."

Unknown

As we explore these five organic representations of when A SHIFT Is Sustained and apply them to our process of *SHIFTING Bravely*, once again we will draw upon testimonies from "A SHIFT In My Life" and from clients' stories. Let's begin exploring each line of the poem.

1) "As you are shifting, you will begin to realize you are not the same person you used to be." (Unknown)

I believe, of the five areas of organic representation, *beginning to realize we are not the same person we used to be,* is one of the most remarkable and meaningful internal rewards of our journey. It is important to note this change may start to show up in little shifts earlier in our seasonal process of self-growth, and this realization can serve as an incredible catalyst as we move through each seasonal phase. However, it is usually much more pronounced after our SHIFT has emerged more fully and has become more thoroughly integrated within our being. Let's take a look at a few examples.

Returning to Annika's story from "A SHIFT In My Life," we recall how she remained committed to recovery from addiction and we learned of her desire to move to Southern California in order to begin her new life. With financial help from her sister, she eagerly embraced the opportunity, securing a position with her same employer. In Annika's words, we witness the extraordinary change in her way of being and in the longevity of it.

I'm almost ten years sober. I am a certified drug and alcohol counselor on a Bachelor's level. I have an awesome career helping others find recovery from whatever it is they are struggling with: alcoholism, other forms of addiction, and eating disorders. I especially love helping women find their way and their own empowerment.

Reading Annika's words brings joy to my heart. We remember as her seeds lay dormant, Annika "managed to destroy her marriage, relationships, trust, and all of her worth and dignity...and was actually shunned by her community due to her behavior while drinking." Grounded in her transformation, Annika not only has advanced her growth—"I am a certified drug and alcohol counselor"—but secure within her strength, she is empowering others to do the same—"I especially love helping women find their way." From being shunned by her community to sharing her wellness with others, Annika's participation in "A SHIFT In My Life," is a testament to her becoming one with her SHIFT. It is validation she is not the person she once was.

In solidifying our transformation, it is the deliberate acknowledgement and affirmation of this new truth—*we are not the same person we used to be*—that sustains us to our new ways of being and strengthens us as we continue to grow.

Similar to Annika's strong emergence and a clear differentiation in her ways of being, we return to Jasmine's story. During her years of dormancy at age nineteen, Jazmine was "living in Hollywood, California, working at a quasi-criminal place (massage parlor) ..." and "where she felt deep disgust with herself after a horrid experience there." After enlisting into the U.S. Army and serving her country, Jazmine's life prior to and after her SHIFT speaks of its authentic growth.

> I served my three years of enlistment and was honorably discharged from the U.S. Army with nice letters and ribbons. Most importantly, as a transformed emotionally healthier and wiser person, I also began to utilize my benefits—the G.I. Education Bill—as I needed the extra money for going to school.
>
> I am able to look upon my degrees as a Licensed Marriage and Family Therapist, a Licensed Clinical Counselor, a certified hypnotist, and a Doctorate in Clinical Psychology, as well as a fulling career as a Clinical Counselor for Veterans, only because of the service in the U.S. Army. I am filled with gratitude for thinking about what would have happened to me if not for the 'shift' the military and 12 Step Program brought me.

It is important to note how Jazmine attributes her strong psychological wellbeing—"a transformed emotionally healthier and wiser person"—as the catalyst for ongoing growth. It is then because of her intentional choices and actions where she began to fuel and strengthen her emergence. After her SHIFT, she proudly claimed evidence of her transformation—"I am able to look upon my degrees...as well as a fulfilling career as a Clinical Counselor for Veterans."

And although Jazmine credits the military and 12-Step program for bringing her shift "to" her, she chose to trust in her journey and to grow within it. By realizing she was "not the same person she used to be," Jazmine recognized her sense of fulfillment and affirmed herself for achieving it.

In making a before-and-after comparison around our shifting process, not only is it important to recognize the major changes in our lives, but it is equally important to acknowledge how our SHIFT is evidenced in other perhaps more subtle areas of our lives as well. In Enrique's story from "A SHIFT In My Life," we recall how health issues developed after years of working tirelessly in two demanding areas of psychology, a psychotherapist and a professor at a local university. After Enrique's SHIFT emerged and his health improved, he peacefully and eagerly embraced his retirement—"I also finally got the message I was OK financially and wouldn't really need to work ever again."

Returning to his story, we see how Enrique's SHIFT is becoming one with him as his strength spills into his spiritual rituals and his personal relationships.

> I grew up in a fairly religious family and had been involved in religious groups for most of my life. At almost the same time [as my shift continued to strengthen], I found and started attending a spiritual group. I know this sounds 'so religious,' but this group was better than any previous one. It was incredibly positive and healthy. My partner and I look forward to church-related activities.
>
> I have made other changes. I have allowed some older 'friendships' to drift away. I have claimed other new friendships, ones I want to support and foster.

Evidence in the sustainability of Enrique's SHIFT is displayed in his newly-discovered discerning beliefs and choices: "I found and started attending a spiritual group which was incredibly positive and healthy..." and, "... I have allowed some older 'friendships' to drift away...and claimed other new friendships." And while acknowledgment of these transformations are meaningful examples of inner personal change and of Enrique's insight that he is not the same person he used to be, they also cross over into the second area of organic strength.

> 2) "The things you used to tolerate have become intolerable." (Unknown)

Over the years in my work with clients as well as in my own recovery, I have utilized this behavioral representation as a strong indicator of an emerging new "self." However, it is when we intentionally implement boundaries, mindfully readjust our expectations, and selectively invest into other people and things, that our *knowing* solidifies itself in strength.

One of the most profound examples of when "The things you used to tolerate have become intolerable" is evidenced in Naomi's story from "A SHIFT In My Life." Returning to her story in Chapter Six, A SHIFT Faces Recurring Resistance, we recall how Naomi's seeds of codependency around her daughter's addiction were awakened and how she paid attention to them. As her shift began emerging, Naomi unearthed another seed of mother wounding. She traveled to Sedona, Arizona, attending a personal retreat where she was able to unearth the betrayals of her unloving mother, and her struggle to survive, and the uncovering of masks she had placed on herself in order to survive.

Joining her in this phase of Summer Strong, we witness how Naomi's shift is sustained within its strength. Her *knowing* speaks for itself.

> The outcome of this dark time eleven years ago is the emergence of an emotionally healthy woman. I learned who I truly am in this lifetime.
>
> My obstacles of dealing with my toxic mother are still here; however, I have learned to stay true to my boundaries and that none of my past was my fault. It was my mother's baggage and it was not mine to carry.
>
> It is so unfortunate that my dad passed away seven months ago. I had hoped my relationship with my mother might have a chance, but she defaulted to her toxic behaviors. I will not tolerate it.
>
> No matter how hard it is to tell her I am not available for her, I am my own woman now.

Naomi's powerful story reveals two important lessons, when A SHIFT Is Sustained.

First, boundary work is hard and it is necessary for our protection. Naomi's boundaries speak to this—"No matter how hard it is to tell her, I am not available for her." Just like the novice gardener who inserted stakes into the ground and draped netting over her beds of growth to protect against external forces of resistance, we too must implement boundaries in our relationships to safeguard ours. Naomi's actions—"I have learned to stay true to my boundaries"—demonstrate her respect for her growth as well as her protection of it—"I will not tolerate it [unhealthy behavior]."

Second, Naomi also teaches us how boundaries create space for truth to thrive. Without chronic or episodic exposure to toxic interference, our *knowing* grounds us and sustains us. Naomi's truths flourish in this strength—"...none of my past was my fault. It was my mother's baggage and it was not mine to carry." Naomi's most revealing truth showcases the extraordinary beauty of its sustainability—"I am my own woman now."

In addition to boundary implementation, A SHIFT Is Sustained by our mindful readjusting of expectations and selective investing into other people and things. Although letting go of unhealthy relationships is frequently necessary, there are other times when we can navigate them without diminishing our strength.

However, it is important to be brutally honest about how our expectations of any relationship might impact us and we must be intentional about our degree of investment.

Returning to Suzanne's story from Chapter Six, A SHIFT Faces Recurring Resistance, we remember her pain of a public shaming and years of alcoholism. We recall how after she paid attention to her seed's calling and tended to them, her SHIFT emerged more fully. She acknowledged and identified her codependency, behaviors which were depleting and draining. After she began setting boundaries, Suzanne also experienced external sources of resistance from family, co-workers, and a few friends. She remained strong.

Picking up with Suzanne's story, we see how she is safeguarding her truths while maintaining personal and professional relationships. From our most recent sessions, she disclosed the following.

"I'm grateful I set really strong boundaries around several of my relationships, especially a couple of them at my work. During this time when there hasn't been much communication with them, I have been able to step back and ask myself, 'What is it that I want from the relationship?' It's strange...I've discovered I feel so much better being out of a close relationship with them, that I really don't want very much more. And.... I have come to understand how they just really are not capable of giving to the relationship in healthy ways.

"So, because I want to work in an environment free of friction, I'm trying out a few different approaches. It's important for me to be respectful and kind. But I don't need to offer to help with things like I did before. Also, I'm keeping my conversations polite and short. If any drama starts up, I excuse myself and walk away."

Suzanne smiled and added, "Oh, and in the morning when I come into work, I readjust my expectations and remind myself of my reality. It keeps me from being disappointed or discouraged. In fact, I've been feeling very content."

One of the beautiful takeaways from Suzanne's story is how her profound *knowing* of what she will tolerate and what she will not, serves as an internal compass as she redefines her levels of investment into relationships—"I've discovered I feel so much better being out of a close relationship with them, that I really don't want much more." This acute awareness also guides Suzanne as she shores up boundaries—"If any drama starts, I excuse myself and walk away."

And this lesson is most important. By adjusting her expectations and reminding herself of her reality, Suzanne remains tethered to her authentic way of being—"I want to work in an environment free of friction" and "I've been feeling very content."

Let's continue to explore additional hallmarks of when A SHIFT Is Sustained. During my first reading of the poem that spoke to me about Summer Strong, I felt that the third and fourth lines of organic representation were in opposition to one another.

> "When you once remained quiet, you are now speaking your truth."
> "Where you once battled and argued, you are now choosing to remain silent."

But on closer examination, I realized they are not. And, each is vitally important to our *knowing*. Let's examine line three.

> 3) "When you once remained quiet, you are now speaking your truth." (Unknown)

Discovering our truths is hard work. Speaking about them can be excruciatingly difficult. As we have witnessed from the stories in "A SHIFT In My Life" as well as in the clients' stories, there was almost always a tremendous amount of shame, secrecy, and stigma embedded within their personal histories and life messages.

And, even after our SHIFT has emerged, there is no guarantee we will not be further shamed, blamed, or judged for speaking our truths. There is always some degree of risk in sharing them.

Therefore, it is important to understand this. I believe you will *know* when you are ready to speak your truths. That *knowing* will show up in one or more of the following ways:

- You will do so when you feel it is safe.
  Speaking your truth might take place in a therapeutic setting; a 12 Step Program; a treatment center; or with a trusted friend, family member, sponsor or mentor.

- You will do so when your truth is calling you to do so.
  Speaking your truth may be an integral part of your growing or recovering process. Not doing so may stifle or arrest your emergence and its sustainability.

- You will speak your truth when you no longer can tolerate not doing so.
  This comes with time and with increasing strength. You will not be able to ignore it. There will be a force or movement within you that cannot be contained any longer. It feels like it must come out or it is going to burst.

- You will do so when you find a comfortable and inviting format or avenue for expressing your truth.
  It might be writing in a journal; speaking with a therapist, counselor or confidant; participating in a group; or practicing any kind of creative expression. Speaking your truth might take place in a public setting or within a private setting such as during meditation, prayer, or spiritual practice.

The participants of "A SHIFT In My Life," were once quiet, but they decided to speak their truths. How did they *know* they were ready? In my correspondence with each of the participants prior to and after receiving their stories, the participants individually acknowledged one or more of the following:

- Feeling safe given the anonymity provided (names would be changed).

- Writing down their stories for an informal study and sharing them publicly advanced their SHIFTS and strengthened their growth.

- No longer being the persons they used to be, the participants responded enthusiastically to the "Letter of Invitation." Voicing their truths could no longer be contained.

- Writing down their stories by answering a few questions, in a private setting and given ample time, was a comfortable format.

And lastly, in examining this hallmark of organic strength, we must embrace a steadfast mindset.

Speaking our truths is not about how others will receive them. Speaking our truths is about us—validating our growth's sustainability by affirming that we are rooted in our truths.

Let's further our understanding of speaking our truths by exploring the meanings behind line four and its implications for us.

4) "Where you once battled and argued, you are now choosing to remain silent." (Unknown)

This fourth organic representation of strength is indeed remarkable. At first read, it may seem as though we are being asked to restrain from speaking our truths. But it is not.

I believe that when we are truly grounded in our growth and its strength, we are at peace with ourselves and with others. Battles or arguments we had within ourselves and with others in proving our truths or substantiating our growth are no longer important. They are no longer necessary. In our peace, we are choosing to silence past representations such as anger, resentment, and blame. Because of our growth, we are choosing to honor it in healthy ways. In doing so, we find ourselves once again taking on the posture of a gardener: being still, listening, staying open, and giving ourselves time for further internal strengthening.

Several of the most beautiful examples of this posturing is evident in Margot's story from "A SHIFT In My Life." We recall how Margot has emerged from a very dysfunctional family of origin and a lengthy unhealthy marriage. With time and hard work, she has broken free from destructive and debilitating shaming life messages, replacing them with empowering truths—"I am not what happened to me. I am what I chose to become."

In Chapter Six, A SHIFT Faces Recurring Resistance, Margot continued strengthening her emergence by "reading and learning about healthier ways of becoming emotionally stronger..." and by "continuing with therapy." And, even as she faced internal forces of resistance, Margot began assuming an inward learning and listening posture of a gardener—"I have spent time quietly observing others...By learning to listen to others, it has calmed my anxiety."

As we return to her story, we witness an inner silence—a growing peace—within her and with others.

> Over time, I recognized some of the good qualities I had gained due to the bad things that had happened to me. From shyness, I learned to reach out in small ways to others who were reticent or fearful, giving them encouragement, recognition, and support.
>
> I began thinking about why my parents acted as they did. Because of their backgrounds, biology, and not knowing any better, I came to a better understanding of others who were not kind or who did harmful things. It never excused their actions, but I gained more empathy for them.
>
> My previous depression, abuse, and loneliness helped me to grow my compassion for others. I knew how horrible and hopeless life could be, and as I grew more confident, I learned ways to help support others while taking care of myself.
>
> After my children were grown, I moved to where I had always wanted to live, in sunshine and warmth. I pursued further education, my career, hobbies, and passions. I now believe I have grown into a person who has a lot to give.
>
> I am basically happy, even when living in difficult circumstances. I have healthy relationships with others and my life partner. I feel confident and I like myself.
>
> And, I am now grateful for all of the loneliness, bad experiences, depression, and hurt I lived with for so long. Without it, I would not be the person I am today.

From Margot's story, we are moved by her quiet, brave persona and its power in sustaining her SHIFT. There are several important lessons to glean from her growth and transformation.

First, Margot gave herself ample time for internal strengthening— "Over time, I recognized some of the good qualities I had gained due to the bad things that had happened to me." When we are in the beginning phases of our seasonal process, it is common and understandable to be angry, argumentative, and reactive, especially to those who have contributed to our wounding. However, as more time passes and we begin to realize we are not the same person we used to be, we also begin reframing our perceptions to reflect our current truths. This does not minimize the harm others have caused. However, this hurt no longer holds us hostage to them. Margot's peace reflects this shift in her truths— "I came to a better understanding of others who were not kind or who did harmful things. It never excused their actions...but I gained more empathy for them."

Second, like a skilled gardener, Margot tethered herself to her organic strength by staying open to receiving new lessons and acquiring new knowledge. As she began thinking about why "my parents acted as they did," and how her "previous depression, abuse, and loneliness helped her to grow her compassion for others," Margot did not get bitter. She got better.

When we remain open to new discoveries and insights regarding our experiences, our defensive posture takes a back seat to welcoming in an understanding of them. It is with deeper insight we find ourselves remaining silent within, settling into our peace and calm.

Lastly and so importantly, Margot displays the skill of a gardener through the difficult posture of being still—"I am basically happy, even when living in difficult circumstances."

When A SHIFT Is Sustained, we are anchored in our truths. And when the waters around us are unpredictable or choppy, our *knowing* of our truths secures us. We do not react to our unsafe environments or adversaries. Where we "once battled and argued," we are now "choosing to remain silent." We now choose a peaceful response.

And, when we maintain the posture of a gardener by sustaining our growth in healthy ways, we affirm "we are rooted in our truth and our truth is allowed to shift and transform" (Unknown). As Margot states so powerfully, "And, I am now grateful for all of the loneliness, bad experiences, depression, and hurt I have lived with so long." Firmly grounded in her truth, Margot further validates her transformation— "Without it, I would not be the person I am today."

We have come to understand that when A SHIFT Is Sustained, there will be evidence of it. We will not be the persons we used to be, things once tolerated will no longer be tolerable, and when and how we speak about ourselves and our truths will mirror an internal representation of lasting strength.

As we examine the fifth hallmark of sustainability, it appears to be a summation of the prior four areas; however, there are several unique distinctions. Let's take a closer look at line five of the poem.

> 5) "You are beginning to understand the value of your voice and there are some situations which no longer deserve your time, energy, and focus." (Unknown)

In honoring our voices and affirming ourselves, we have learned the importance of speaking our truths and of presenting them in ways representative of sustainable growth. As we begin to understand the *value* of our voice, we begin to embrace a deeply insightful and intentional posture of a gardener. It is one that requires quiet perseverance, a steady stream of resilience, and endless patience. With continual growth and increased internalization of our truths, it is a posture that displays an inner core of self-compassion, discernment, and self-empowerment.

During this phase of Summer Strong, it is one where the Flower found herself calling upon her truths and trusting in their sustainability.

Returning to the Flower's story in Chapter Six, we recall her courageous character as she continued to face external and internal recurring forces of resistance. We remember her commitment to overcoming forms of melancholy in her places of employment and in her inner personal work within our therapeutic relationship. As the Flower's emergence strengthened, her voice spoke her truths—"I definitely am becoming the person I am meant to be."

And yet, we recall how the Flower faced a deeply personal and painful challenge. Her partner, her beloved tall slender Birch, was "adrift... numbing his pain." Her words to him spoke of the Flower's internalization of her truths—"God brought me a 'gift', not a drunk. You need to decide which one you want to be." As our sessions continued, the Flower continued to *voice her value* as she embraced a posture of self-compassion, discernment, and self-empowerment.

After eighteen months together, I observed how the Flower was becoming accustomed to *being the person she is meant to be*. She became protective of it and readily embraced a practice previously foreign to her—one of self-compassion. This self-love showed up in several areas of her life.

In one of our sessions, she revealed the following.

"Work has been really hard lately. There are so many new programs to learn on the computer and I'm not getting it fast enough. My supervisor has been pretty tough on me. But I know she cares about me and just wants me to succeed. And... I know I'm really hard on myself."

I nodded. The Flower smiled and continued.

"I'm proud of myself though.... I 'know' I am learning to trust in myself and in others at work. And, I'm doing what we practiced. I'm reframing my supervisor as my 'mentor' and learning from her. I no longer put myself down for what I don't know. I am confident in the gifts

I bring to the job—gifts others don't have. I 'know' I am making a difference with our clients."

The Flower's words portray so beautifully how she is *voicing her value*. Prior to her shift, she was extremely self-critical and self-deprecating. As part of her self-compassion, she is learning to be kinder to herself. She is liking herself. She is recognizing she is worthy of her self-love—"I 'know' I am making a difference with our clients."

The Flower also demonstrated her self-compassion by making her self-care a priority. This was extremely difficult for her as she found meaning and purpose in giving out to others first. However, once she had experienced who *she was meant to be,* she strongly implemented her self-care practices. She proudly reported them to me as our sessions continued.

"I'm taking care of a number of doctor's appointments. Things I've let slide for a while but I know they are important. It feels good to take control of my health..."

As I normally did, I checked in about her daily practices. She eagerly responded.

"Oh yes, I'm getting plenty of sleep...and good deep sleep. It's sort of late when I get home, but I am eating well and getting some exercise at work.

"Sometimes on the weekends, I wish I could do more. But, I'm tired from the week. I'm not as keen on having visitors as I used to...I just want to relax."

The Flower let out a soft laugh and added, "I know what you're going to say, Holli. 'If it's important to me, I'll do it.' And, I'm gonna!"

While we talked about the Flower's self-compassion, I would often move into a tender area of discussion but one of equal importance—her relationship with the tall silver Birch. Over the past few months, there had been good communication between them and an understanding of acceptable and unacceptable behaviors. More importantly, the Flower continued to strengthen a key area of self-love—respecting herself, her truths, and her voice.

During a sensitive session, the Flower disclosed her feelings of self-respect.

"Now that I 'know' who I am, I respect who I am. I am not perfect, nobody is. I also know that part of respecting myself is not allowing others to disrespect me, no matter who it is. Not my mother, not other family members, and...not my 'man'."

The Flower took in a deep breath and then exhaled. She relaxed and spoke. "I've talked with my 'man' about the couple-care exercises you suggested. He's been willing to do some of them. And...they're helping."

And with steady strength in her voice, the Flower added, "I told him, 'As long as we're moving forward, I'm good. I'm just not going backwards.'"

Quite often, I will hear from clients, "Holli, isn't self-compassion just being selfish?" Or, "Gosh, self-love sounds so self-centered."

My response is rooted in this truth. The degree we love ourselves, take care of ourselves, and respect ourselves is a predictor to the degree others will do the same. In other words, how well we treat ourselves will teach others how to treat us. Others will not love us unconditionally if we do not love ourselves first.

Along with learning to love herself, the Flower supported her worth by taking care of herself—"It feels good to take control of my health..." And just as importantly, through bravely practicing self-respect, the Flower determined what she would accept and what she wouldn't—"As long as we're moving forward, I'm good. I'm just not going backwards."

Over the next couple of months, the Flower's organic strength continued to flourish. However, she reported to me that the spirit world was warning her that something bad was going to happen. She began preparing by stocking up on food and other necessities, not just for herself but for others in need. Within several weeks, the world pandemic was landing on the shores of the United States. Although I was concerned about all of my clients, I felt confident in the Flower's sustainability in moving through the crisis.

During our first session via teletherapy after our state's shutdown, the Flower maintained a gardener's posture of perseverance as she embraced the second area of *understanding the value of her* voice—discernment.

"I think I told you that the spirit world had sent me a message. And, I trust in their messages, whether they are good or not. I also know I will remain open to what this time has in store for me. I do want to help."

The Flower hesitated, then added, "Yes, I will take care of myself first."

Over the next several months, the Flower worked remotely from home. Her job duties changed, but they were more meaningful and rewarding than her previous duties at work. Finding more time for herself and wanting to serve in areas of need, the Flower searched for ways to help her community while staying safe. She carefully assessed the needs most close to home and to her heart, investing into those she felt deserving.

"Through my job and with my own resources, I've been able to find a way to help hurting families, not just in my town but in a few surrounding areas. Because I know what it is like to go without food, my 'roots of compassion' are telling me this is what I want and need to do."

It is important to integrate into our being that the more secure we are in ourselves and our truths, the more discerning we become. First, in our discernment we are clear about who to trust and who not to. The Flower's words portray this so powerfully as she welcomes those from the spirit world who speak to her—"And, I trust in their messages, whether they are good or not."

Second, like a gardener whose deep *knowing* fosters precision in decision-making, our internalized *knowing* focuses our thinking and behaviors. The Flower states beautifully, "Because I know what it is like to go without food, my 'roots of compassion' are telling me this is what I want and need to do."

Third, the posture of discernment comes with time, experience, patience, and resilience. It cannot be rushed. However, it *will* show itself. We *will* feel it. We *will* act on it. The more internalized our truths become, the more we will be able to discern who or what is deserving of our voice, time, energy, and focus. And, like the Flower, we will be secure in our actions—"...my 'roots of compassion' are telling me this is what I want and need to do."

As the first few months of the pandemic brought additional challenges, the Flower's self-compassion practices and her keen levels of discernment deepened as she continued to sustain her growth. Integrating more strongly the areas of speaking her truth and of its peaceful presentation into her new ways of being, the Flower's voice was truly becoming an organic representation of its sustainability. The first few months also brought along with it a sort of honeymoon period, not just for the Flower personally but also with her tall slender silver Birch. During one of our sessions, she spoke of this time as one of ease and comfort.

"It's been so nice to be home again. Without the commute and the long work hours, I'm finding I am getting better rest and I am more relaxed. I'm kinda liking this remote work schedule.

"And, I've been thinking about this...When I was forced to take a leave from my job, I felt like such a failure and I felt so much shame. But this time...it's completely different. This was not my choosing. This was not my fault. And so, I'm just able to enjoy the freedom of it...not carrying that burden. And, this time... I am a different person."

I smiled and validated the Flower. And then, I gently inquired about her 'man.'

"He's been good. I think he's really liked having me home again. He still likes taking care of me...and because my job responsibilities at work keep changing, there are some things he's been helping me with—the sort of 'heavy lifting' of stuff... like getting resources to folks."

She paused and continued.

"There have been a few times when I have had to talk to my 'man' about boundaries regarding relationships with his family. And I'm sensing that with the 'stay in place' recommendations, he's getting a little restless...But we're managing and we're still communicating well..."

Rooted in her truth, the Flower added, "It's just clear to me how I am becoming stronger in my role in the relationship...in having a say about who and what we invite into our lives."

As I listened to the Flower, I could hear another strength showing up, one of self-empowerment. Because the word empowerment has many connotations and interpretations, it is important to clarify its usage. In our understanding and application of it, empowerment means *valuing our voice* by *voicing our value.* In other words, self-empowerment shows up as clear, confident, authentic representations of our truths and our growth. When we are *valuing our voice,* we do not seek to dominate or demand. And when we are *voicing our value,* we do so by representing our strong beliefs in who we are as we thoughtfully and respectfully conduct our lives. In the Flower's words, "It's just clear to me how I am becoming stronger in my role in the relationship...in having a say about who and what we invite into our lives."

A month passed until our next teletherapy session. I was looking forward to it. As soon as the Flower spoke, there was a change in her voice and in her.

"Holli, shortly after our last session, my 'man' started drinkin' again...but more this time. And when he drinks, he gets so angry—not at me but at the world. I know his abusive past is 'right behind him'—in his thoughts. A couple of weeks ago, he had one really bad episode. I took care of myself...but the next day, I had a talk with him."

Over the next several minutes, the Flower explained the boundaries she readjusted and shored up. She made it crystal clear what she would accept and what she would not. She laid out the options for her 'man' if things continued the way they were. And then, with a confidence, a clarity, and an authenticity I had never before been witness to in a nearly two-year journey together, the Flower's proclamation of self-love and self-empowerment came forth.

"I told my 'man,' 'You cut yourself and you expect me to bleed. But there is a rising up of who I am as a core person. I recognize I am stronger. I will help reclaim you but I will not be your stalwart'."

And with one final statement, the Flower *voiced her value.*

"I'm becoming who I am meant to be."

As the Flower spoke, the space between us filled with her truths. They could not be contained. Her self-empowerment was a testament to when A SHIFT Is Sustained. Her words signified its legitimacy—"There is a rising up of who I am as a core person."

It is when our SHIFT solidifies within us, that we find ourselves unable, unwilling, and incapable of compromising our truths or our ways of being. It is simply non-negotiable as we are rooted in our truths. In the Flower's words, "I'm becoming who I am meant to be."

The beauty of this phase of Summer Strong is that even though the season comes to an end, our organic areas of growth do not. This is who *we* are now. This is what we claim.

- We no longer are the same person

- We no longer tolerate the intolerable

- We speak our truths

- We speak with a peaceful spirit

- We value of our voice by voicing our value

And, as we anticipate Autumn Splendor, we also claim that although we are "rooted in our truths, our truths are allowed to shift and transform." For we have come to understand how *SHIFTING* is dynamic. It is not stagnant. And in our desire to continue growing, we must return to and rely upon the posture of a gardener. With quiet perseverance, a steady stream of resilience, and endless patience, we must move with the seasons and the changes they bring.

As the Flower and I marked our two-year anniversary together, I observed as she continued "to shift and transform." And still, because Autumn is a season of planning and preparing for future growth, I wondered where her path would lead her next.

Would she choose to move through Autumn Splendor, solo and secure in her truths?

What other insights might surface, changing the trajectory of her growth?

And would the tall slender silver Birch sacrifice all that was good in his life? Or would he courageously embrace his own seasonal process of self-growth?

Exercises—A SHIFT Is Sustained

In the second phase of Summer Strong, we learned the following:

> Moving into the fullness of Summer Strong, we claim our strength. One of the beautiful gifts of *SHIFTING Bravely* is *knowing* how our growth is capable of sustaining us. Our *knowing* is evidenced by a clear differentiation between our truths about ourselves and our ways of being prior to our SHIFT in comparison to during and after our SHIFT. These new truths show up in our attitudes, beliefs, and feelings as well as our actions, behaviors, and choices.
>
> We also learned it is important to acknowledge and affirm the embodiments of our strength and to recognize the evidence of our growth. In doing so, not only do we validate our seasonal process of self-growth, but we also empower ourselves *knowing* A SHIFT Is Sustained.

Take as much time as needed as you complete these exercises. Enjoy the rewards of your hard work. As you continue down your path of growth, healing, and transformation, bask in the glow of your "new self."

1. In order to acknowledge evidence of strength and sustainable growth, we explored five areas of organic representation. Take your time and reflect carefully upon the following five areas. Then, choose which representations apply to you. For each one, describe in detail and explain fully how its sustainability is showing up for you. This is a time to validate your process of self-growth and to empower yourself in its legitimacy and its longevity.

    ➤ As you are shifting, you will begin to realize you are not the same person you used to be.

    ➤ The things you used to tolerate have become intolerable.

    ➤ When you once remained quiet, you are now speaking your truth.

    ➤ Where you once battled and argued, you are now choosing to remain silent.

> ➤ You are beginning to understand the value of your voice and there are some situations which no longer deserve your time, energy, and focus.

2. In A SHIFT Is Sustained, whose story connected with you? Why? What are you learning about your "new self"? How does it feel?

3. At the end of A SHIFT Is Sustained, you are reminded that although you are rooted in your truths, "your truths are allowed to shift and transform." How does this feel for you? How are you approaching your next season of growth—Autumn Splendor?

Season Four:
Autumn Splendor

8 A SHIFT Cultivates Future Growth

"We all change colors and lose our leaves...Then we bloom again."

Maria Lago

Throughout the prior seasons of *SHIFTING Bravely*, we have been called upon to work really hard. As a result of our investments into Winter Stillness, Spring Stirrings, and Summer Strong, we have experienced tremendous growth and have been integrating its transformation fully into our lives. Autumn Splendor is a time to soak in the beauty and peace of our new growth and to partake in the harvest of our newly formed emergence. And although this is a time for celebration, it is also one of quiet reflection and self-examination. It is one of well-earned affirmation and hope-filled projection. For it is the discerning gardener who learns from past seasons and prepares for the future. It is the wise gardener who understands A SHIFT Cultivates Future Growth.

My daughter, who took on the role of a gardener last winter and spring, was no different. And after a summer of standing strong against recurring environmental forces of resistance, the garden beds carefully nurtured by their caring gardener continued to produce into Autumn. As the rains announced the ending of harvest time, the attentive gardener began clearing away the remnants of plants and the scatterings of leaves. During the cleansing process, the mindful gardener took stock of what she had learned and what she would do differently next season. She also conducted an honest inventory of what had served her well and what practices she would continue to implement.

During Autumn Splendor, we must take time to reflect upon self-growth and closely take stock of all phases of our process. First, this is a time for us to look back, glean from what we have learned, and make adjustments or changes for the ensuing season. Second, it is also a time to celebrate our successes, identify what worked well, and plan for future growth.

Let's begin by taking a look back at all phases of our seasonal process of growth. Although you will be provided time at the end of this chapter to respond more thoroughly, begin thinking about the following questions.

- What areas of SHIFTING were most challenging to me? Why?

- In which phases of SHIFTING was I most vulnerable? Why?

- Are there specific conditions or circumstances of SHIFTING when I am more likely to struggle? If so, explain in detail.

Write down anything that surfaces as you are pondering these questions. Don't dismiss it or minimize it. If it is coming up, it is probably important. Each of us is unique in our process and in our areas of vulnerability. Honor what is true for you.

Although ALL phases of the seasonal process are important, based on my experience as a therapist as well as what has been shared in the stories from "A SHIFT In My Life," I believe there are three phases within our process where we tend to be more vulnerable or where there may be more of a struggle or challenge.

1. A SHIFT Lies Dormant

2. A SHIFT Takes Root

3. A SHIFT Faces Recurring Resistance

In order to Cultivate Future Growth, let's briefly re-examine the importance of each of these three phases. And, let's see what more we can learn as we enter Autumn Splendor and soak in the dynamic beauty of this season—"We all change colors, lose our leaves....and then bloom again." (Lago)

A SHIFT Lies Dormant

It is often the case when clients enter into Autumn Splendor and just when they are beginning to experience the joy of a whole new way of being, they will stumble into the quicksand of regret. I will know it instantly by their sinking words, "If only I had done this work sooner." Or, "I should have done this years ago...I've wasted so much of my life." Or, "If I had my life to do over, I would..." Instead of beating themselves up, I ask clients to look back and reflect upon the reasons why their seeds were in their dormant states.

During this period of self-examination, I ask clients to recall their forms of camouflage, to name them, and to conduct periodic inventories on the degree of their presence or interference in their lives. By conducting this intentional practice, we position ourselves more intuitively—paying attention to an awakening of seeds during our next season of growth.

At the end of this chapter in the Topics for Journaling, you will be asked to re-examine your forms of camouflage and assess your levels of vulnerability. For now, spend a few moments thinking about the following questions.

What *internal* forms of camouflage tend to pull me away from staying true to myself and my growth? How can I follow through with my commitment to confronting and managing them?

What *external* forms of camouflage tend to pull me away from staying true to myself and my growth? How can I follow through with my commitment to confronting and managing them?

Although numerous forms of camouflage were discussed in Chapter One, the presence of shaming life messages is perhaps the most destructive force moving against future growth. We recall in the stories from Suzanne, Britt, Phillip, Margo, Naomi, Jazmine, and others, how their shaming self-messages of worthlessness, inadequacy, and a lack of mattering impacted their lives with severe pain and disturbance, both psychologically and physically. And, we remember how they worked tirelessly throughout the phases of self-growth to release their injurious messages, reclaim themselves, and replace their toxicity with self-affirming messages of value, being enough, and belonging.

Returning to Britt's story from "A SHIFT In My Life," we recall how she internalized destructive shaming messages from her mother and sister as she "would always be a failure..." and that "...others would have to rescue her from her inadequacies." In Chapter Six, A SHIFT Faces Recurring Resistance, Britt's words revealed her emerging self.

> I am more finely attuned to manipulation by others, by those who would steal the power of someone who is vulnerable to enrich themselves. I have learned to embrace the fear and move through it...

And yet, as we revisit Britt's final words in her story, we witness how she beautifully prepares for future growth while treating herself compassionately and gently.

> Sometimes I have to laugh at myself as I realize I have just succumbed to the same darn thing [life messages of a fear of failure] I thought I had processed and put to rest. But then, I realize it has appeared in a slightly different guise.
>
> But each time this takes place, I learn more and am better prepared to work through the challenges life presents me.

It is important to remain aware of all insidious forms of camouflage and to remind ourselves of their relentless nature. Like a purposeful gardener, we must stay attuned to their presence and attentive to their possible interference. Just as Britt is doing, as we prepare and plan for future growth, it is important to arrest the intrusions of camouflage in a timely manner and in tender ways. We see how Britt has embraced humor rather than succumbing to fear as she moves through her area of vulnerability—those nasty life messages: "Sometimes I have to laugh at myself as I realize I have just succumbed to the same darn thing...But each time this takes place, I learn more and am better prepared." More importantly, because Britt chooses to learn from challenging areas, she is positioned precisely for cultivating future growth.

During this season of reflection and self-examination it is also important to revisit another susceptible phase of emergence from Chapter Four.

A SHIFT Takes Root

During and after her first harvest, the mindful gardener reflected on what went well and what didn't. And what changes, if any, she would make for the next growing season. Her period of self-examination led to the following conclusions. The bounty of vegetables produced was beyond the gardener's wildest expectations. Aside from planting a few less tomato plants, there would be one major adjustment in preparing the soil for the ensuing planting season.

In a few of the planter beds, the gardener used a combination of straw and soil. The vegetables planted in those beds did grow, but their size dwarfed in comparison to those in a mixture of different combinations of clay, sand, and silt. Upon closer examination, the gardener learned how the roots were not able to grow to their full potential due to the thick, hardened nature of the straw. Without a porous consistency, their growth was stunted as were the stems, leaves, and vegetables. Needless to say, for the next season, straw would be eliminated.

In Chapter Four, A SHIFT Takes Root, we learned the importance of conducting ongoing examination and preparation of our soil as well as continual assessment of its environment. During Autumn Splendor, we must adapt the same intentional posture as that of the gardener.

In reviewing our seasonal process of growth, it is critical we take a brutally honest inventory of our soil's condition, what areas were not as strong or healthy, and where there may need to be minor adjustments or major changes.

As we reflect upon our soil's constitution and re-examine its porous nature, we want to revisit some of the following considerations. There will be time for further exploration at the end of the chapter. For now, think through these and write down anything that surfaces.

Are there any additional underlying issues, injuries, or injustices clogging up my soil? If so, identify them.

During the critical phase of when A SHIFT Takes Root, did I discover anything else that may interfere with or stunt my growth as I move forward? If so, explain.

What am I still carrying around or spending negative energy on that may be contaminating my soil and restricting future growth? Explain.

Did I learn anything about my roots that surprised me or I didn't expect? Explain.

During Autumn Splendor, there is no shame in identifying or rediscovering areas of needed attention. There is only disappointment if we are not observant and open to these vulnerable areas. Looking forward to the next season, we view increasing our awareness and knowledge of our soil's composition as powerful companions for expanding our growth, not just regarding current vulnerabilities but on emerging ones as well.

Returning to Robert's story, we remember how he fell in love with teaching and learning, put all his energies into education, and in his words, "a whole new direction and life opened up for me—a life I had never imagined." In the concluding paragraph of Robert's story from "A SHIFT In My Life," we witness his extraordinary mindful assessment of his roots and their role in expanding his growth.

> Looking back on my SHIFT, I was able to take all the skills I had learned growing up and apply them to future challenges such as building an interdisciplinary, supplemental education and archeological research center.

I had to give up my dream of accruing wealth, but I knew I
had the skills necessary to be economically independent and shift
my focus whenever necessary.

Although Robert's roots were strong and healthy, they presented him
with a unique challenge. They were cultivated to produce an entirely
different outcome—taking over a family business. However, through
purposeful acknowledgment of their strength and endurance, Robert was
not only able to change his career path but also remain open for future
growth opportunities—"I knew I had the skills necessary to be
economically independent and shift my focus whenever necessary."

In addition to A SHIFT Lies Dormant and A SHIFT Takes Root, there
is one more additional phase that warrants re-examination from Chapter
Six.

A SHIFT Faces Recurring Resistance

Assessing and evaluating her first successful season of growth, the
gardener learned much about internal and external recurring resistance.
Although the purposeful gardener was aware she could do nothing
regarding the seasonal fire danger in her mountain community, she was
determined to be more proactive in the protection of her garden,
especially during the adverse environmental forces of Summer Strong.
Therefore, for the upcoming season, it is her intention to install a drip
system. Of course, this will not ward off a raging fire. However, it will
provide a consistent barrier against heat and wind, and it will sustain the
garden not just in her presence but more importantly, in her absence.

As we conduct our self-examination, it is important to remember that
like the wise gardener who is proactively taking measures to secure the
soil's dampness, we must do all we can to safeguard our "new self."
There will always be forces that continue to test and challenge us. Some
of them will be out of our control. The beauty is we will learn from them,
anticipate, and plan accordingly.

In revisiting our *internal* forces of recurring resistance, we want to
keep a pulse on the following areas of vulnerability. As you have done
previously, for now, reflect upon these questions and write down
anything coming up for you.

Am I still struggling with self-doubt or shaming life messages? If so,
describe what is going on for you.

Are there any actions, attitudes, behaviors, thoughts or feelings I tend
to deny, minimize, or rationalize that may inhibit future growth? If so,
describe them and their impact.

In addition to the two adjustments in the soil's composition and its protection against resistance, the intentional gardener was already planning on making one more change for the next season of growth—rotating her crops. Her reasons for doing so were based on well-documented evidence. First, crop rotation helps to maintain soil structure and nutrient levels. Second, crop rotation not only helps to prevent soil-borne pests from getting a foothold in the garden but also aids with weed suppression. In other words, through the rotation of her crops, the gardener was once again being proactive in constructing barriers against future external resistance.

As we continue our self-examination, we must also reflect upon external or environmental factors and their impact on our growth. Although the gardener is able to rotate her crops to maintain healthier conditions for growth, many of us may not be able to or we may not want to move away from or change our environments in order to advance our growth. However, from Chapter Four, we recall how we learned the importance of protecting our growth and nurturing it. Although there were other helpful practices, we came to appreciate how this was accomplished largely through strong boundary work.

Recalling all phases of our seasonal process and re-examining *external* areas of vulnerability or struggle, spend time reflecting upon the following considerations. For now, write down anything coming up for you. We will address this further at the end of the chapter.

- Who or what continues to challenge my growth in ways I find difficult to address? Explain in detail.

- What boundaries did I implement and then let go or back down from? Identify and explain why this happened.

- Where, with whom, and under what circumstances am I most likely not to protect myself and nurture my growth? Why? Explain thoroughly.

- What relationships do I need to withdraw from or end? Why? Explain how they are impacting you.

- What environments do I need to withdraw from or move away from? Why? Explain how they are impacting you.

- What relationships and environments are healthy for my future growth? Identify and explain their influence on you.

In planning for the next season, our degree of future growth is dependent upon the degree of maintaining our soil's healthy structure, its levels of nutrients, and the ongoing implementation of protective boundaries. In my own recovery, in my years of working with clients, and in the stories from "A SHIFT In My Life," I believe that boundary work is one of the hardest skills to integrate into our lives on a consistent basis. And yet, just like crop rotation, it creates a healthy space for expanding present emergence and for cultivating future growth.

Returning to Margot's story from Chapter Seven, A SHIFT Is Sustained, we learned how her life changed after she left her previous environment.

> After I moved to where I had always wanted to live, in sunshine and warmth, I pursued education, my career, hobbies, and passion. I now believe I have grown into a person who has a lot to give...I have healthy relationships with others and my life partner. I feel confident and I like myself.

In one of her concluding paragraphs, I was struck by Margot's words in relationship to her ongoing boundary work and the unforeseen, powerful emergence it brought her.

> By moving away to diverse environments in various states, I was able to experience something I had always yearned for—I met people from all walks of life. Growing up, my family was prejudiced against anyone in a lower class than ours. But I didn't realize it until I got to know more people. The discovery that I could learn from anyone, that everyone had some positive traits, and that I could be friends with anyone was...life-changing.

Margot's story encapsulates an incredibly important takeaway. We learned when crops are rotated, the soil's health is sustained for future growth. If we desire to be proactive in cultivating future growth, it is often necessary that we plant ourselves in different environments, exposing ourselves to healthier nutrients and experiencing the discoveries within. Is it risky? Yes, it is. And yet, in Margot's words, it is well worth it—"The discovery that I could learn from anyone, that everyone had some positive traits, and that I could be friends with anyone was...life-changing."

What a beautiful testament to the power of trusting in our "new self" and in our ongoing process.

During Autumn Splendor, we have come to understand it is important to look back and discover what we want to do differently in order to cultivate future growth. However, it is just as important to celebrate our journey of *SHIFTING Bravely*. It is important to call out our successes and to identify what worked well. It is also critical to affirm ourselves in the process. Let's begin by responding to a few questions.

What areas of *SHIFTING* spoke to you and did you connect with most easily? Name them and explain why.

In which phases of *SHIFTING* did you feel your process really take hold and feel your emergence taking form? Name them. Then, explain and describe.

Are there specific lessons, stories, or approaches that inspired, motivated, or encouraged you in your process? If so, explain or describe.

What insights, lessons or messages will you carry with you in your next season of growth? Explain and describe.

Even if a specific practice or principle worked well for you, is there anything you might want to modify or change with the expectation of how it will augment your future growth? Explain and describe.

Although we will revisit these questions at the end of the chapter, please spend time reflecting upon them and writing down your thoughts. We are more likely to advance our growth if we know in advance what contributes to it.

Along with identifying what has worked well for us, Autumn Splendor is also a time for well-earned affirmation and hope-filled projection. In my work with clients over the years, as well as in my own recovery, I found again and again how we can be our harshest critics. We simply do not take the time to honor and validate the work we have done.

Yes, it is wonderful when someone else takes notice of our "new self" or when we are complimented on our growth. However, we have come to understand how tethering ourselves to external forms of validation is fleeting and often artificial. When we can get comfortable affirming ourselves, we have an honest, authentic, and consistent internal source of inspiration and validation. Our worth and our sense of mattering, and of being enough, comes from within. It is up to us to replenish it. It is how we maintain our truths, sustain our "new self," and cultivate our growth as we move into the next growing season.

Autumn Splendor is perhaps the most peaceful yet purposeful season of all. And yet, it is often underestimated. For its magnificence is showcased in a time of quiet reflection and self-examination. By taking stock of what has and what has not worked well for us, through making minor adjustments and major changes, and by practicing meaningful self-affirmation, we continue on our path. It is a remarkable path of hope, in the present and in the future.

As the Flower entered Autumn Splendor, she too welcomed the time of quiet reflection and self-examination. While external forces of resistance had calmed in the past couple of months, the Flower remained centered in her strong, healthy core, and she continued making boundary-based decisions. Our monthly sessions were filled with deep care and concern for others, but not at the expense of her self-care. In a recent session, the Flower spoke of additional changes and adjustments in her life and in her relationships.

"Holli, my work situation has changed again...although I don't really mind. Because of the pandemic, I'm still going to be working from home a few days a week, but I will now go to the office for just a couple of days. However, I'm being placed at a different location... again. It's sort of interesting looking back at how fearful I was when I returned to work last time. I was so unsure of myself. This time, there is a sense of anticipation...but not a dread. Physically and emotionally, I feel calm. I'm proud of myself and how far I have come..."

I smiled and listened as the Flower shared additional insights into her growth.

"One of the hardest things for me has been setting boundaries...not just with my family but with anyone! But ya know what, I'm getting really good at it!"

The Flower laughed. I joined in. Then, I asked, "Would you share more?"

"Well, you know I've had to set really strong boundaries with my 'man's' family. And I think the thing that has amazed me is how doing so has created room 'for me'...to continue to grow and to just be me. It's sort of hard to explain...but it's like their unhealthiness put barriers around me and held me in it with them. But now, I am the one putting boundaries around myself, and they are adapting to me...or they are not coming around anymore! What I've learned is that boundaries work! What I need to do more of....is not waiting so long before setting them!"

Listening to the Flower, I was struck by her poise and her confidence. With a quiet assuredness, she acknowledged her growth: "It's sort of interesting looking back at how fearful I was when I returned to work last time. I was so unsure of myself. This time, there is a sense of anticipation...but not a dread."

Through her recognition of this previously dominant area of vulnerability, she continues to distance herself from a past shaming life-message, such as "not being enough." More importantly, she is affirming herself in the process—"I'm proud of myself and how far I have come."

From her disclosures, I was also amazed at the Flower's increasing insight into the importance of her boundary work. Because giving to others completely and serving them selflessly has been a lifelong passion and purpose, the practice of setting and maintaining boundaries runs contrary to the Flower's being. However, in her time of reflection, the Flower voiced so beautifully the inner growth she has experienced because of her hard work: "I think the thing that has amazed me is how doing so [boundary setting] has created room 'for me' …to continue to grow and to just be me."

It is important to emphasize that *knowing* what is working for us is critical. *Acknowledging* and *affirming* its benefits condition our soil for future growth.

Our session continued and the Flower shared the ease and comfort within her "new self." I listened and also affirmed her ongoing boundary work with her family and in work-related relationships. Before I asked, the Flower moved into her most personal relationship, that of her 'man.'

"I am feeling better about things… and I'm even feeling hopeful. Over the past couple of months, my 'man' and I have been communicating… more openly and honestly. I haven't held back. He knows what I expect…"

She paused. Then continued. A soft sigh was released followed by a smile.

"We'll sit out on the front porch on the weekends or sometimes on my days working from home. We sip our coffee and just talk. He loves to talk…but it takes time for my 'man' to say the hard stuff. But he's doing it.

He's taking responsibility for his drinkin' and his behaviors. He's owning his moods and taking care of himself when he's out of sorts. And, I've come to understand how this pandemic has really affected him. He told me the other day how he feels restless…like he's being penned in…and he's spending too much time in his head. I get that…But I remind him how even though I know the confinement and all the stress isn't easy for any of us, he knows what he needs to do."

Over the next several minutes, the Flower disclosed specific steps her "man' was taking in accepting responsibility for his thoughts and behaviors. There were times during the past two years of working together when the Flower often shared some of the tools and exercises she was utilizing. Recently, her tall slender Birch was becoming more receptive to them and was willing to try some of them out. She explained how he was identifying his triggers and planning ahead in managing them or working through them. The Flower spoke to her 'man' about "self-checking," and helped him to identify areas of vulnerability or when he felt he was no longer in his "comfort zone." As she continued sharing, I listened intently, honoring the seriousness of our conversation. The Flower's spirited voice resurfaced.

"Holli, I've told my 'man' how my therapy has not only helped me, but it has helped him too!"

Then, the Flower swayed a bit and chuckled, "You're getting two healthier people for the price of one!"

Our laughter softened and we settled back into our session. The Flower continued to share her reflections on her relationship and on her ongoing growth.

"The past two years have taught me so much. I want to share something with you...."

The Flower hesitated, thought for a moment, and then spoke slowly.

"When I first came to see you, I think I mentioned to you that I had read your book *Daughters Betrayed By Their Mothers*....Well, I have to admit when I read it the first time, I was in such a fog. I really didn't remember much of anything. It just didn't stick....But recently, I picked it up again and read it. The whole book. But this time...it all made sense to me. I could see myself in the stories...and it feels so comforting knowing I am not alone."

And, with a growing intensity in her voice, she added, 'Gosh...after all this time, it's amazing to me how I was ready to read the stories and really hear the messages in them. I've thought about how I take things in when I am ready to receive them, and I've learned I have to be patient with myself. The lessons I am supposed to learn will come to me...with time."

While the Flower spoke, I could feel a lump in my throat start to form. Her insights and awareness not only into her growing process but into the seasonal process itself were profoundly moving. The Flower was recognizing and practicing something so many individuals fall short of doing.

As we move through our growing process, we must be patient with ourselves, emerge at our own pace, and always remain open to growth messages coming our way. Early in our process we may not connect with tools, strategies, or lessons. Later, in our time of reflection and self-examination, it is important to return to or revisit prior resources and avenues for support, especially if there is a nudging within us. As the Flower stated so insightfully, "I've thought about how I take things in when I am ready to receive them."

The Flower paused for a moment. Just as I was preparing to ask a follow-up question, she returned the conversation to her tall silver Birch. Her voice remained firm and gentle.

"I know I am not responsible for fixing my 'man.' I know he has to do his own work. And, I understand that I am 'ahead of him'. He has a long way to go…"

The Flower paused again. Her eyes filled with tears. I waited.

"The other day when he and I were talking, he said he feels safe with me…He said he feels loved…."

Her voice quivered.

"He said he feels 'good enough' when he is with me."

I waited.

"I understand how he feels…and what it means to feel safe with someone. I have experienced that in our work together…in our relationship."

The Flower looked at me. Our eyes met. Compassionate regard filled the space between us. "And, I now know what it feels like to become enough…"

I sat quietly, absorbing her words. With a growing sense of hope, she added, "It's just a beginning for him…I know. But it is a beginning."

Before we concluded our session, the Flower glowed within Autumn Splendor by validating herself and affirming her priorities in Cultivating Future Growth.

"No matter what happens, I know that in order to keep myself on my path I have to put myself first. That means….my self-care is my highest priority. I know what it feels like to be strong. I know what it feels like to be healthy."

Her stem erect and her blossom fully open, the Flower boldly spoke her truths, "There is no turning back. Months ago, I said, 'There is a rising up of who I am as a core person'….Today and in the days ahead, I am becoming who I am meant to be. Nothing or no one is going to take that away from me."

Over the next several minutes, I observed the Flower closely. To be honest, it was hard for me to speak. The lump in my throat made it almost impossible to swallow. Tears were burning my eyes as I tried to hold them back. Thinking over our two-year plus journey, I was overwhelmed with the Flower's passage moving through discomfort and listening to her now. Instead of me guiding the session, the Flower was teaching me who she was and who she is still becoming. I had the privilege of bearing witness to her transformation. It is something I will always cherish.

The Flower maintains her monthly sessions with me. It is part of her self-care. It is part of her growing process. Recently, she shared how she is looking ahead to changing colors, losing her leaves, and blooming again. Instead of differing work responsibilities and roles being imposed upon her, the Flower is proactively seeking out other options and opportunities. With a preliminary plan already in place, she is anticipating major shifts and transformations in the next season of growth, not just in her professional life but other areas as well. She is poised for their awakening and positioned for paying attention to them. Like a well-seasoned gardener, the Flower is confident, courageous and committed as she tends to all phases of their emergence. Like a humble gardener, she will remain open to learning from them.

And the tall silver slender Birch? He is presently on his own path of *SHIFTING Bravely*. And, he is at the Flower's side.

Exercises—A SHIFT Cultivates Future Growth

Moving into Autumn Splendor, we have learned it is… "a time of celebration and a time of quiet reflection and self-examination. It is a time of well-earned affirmation and hope-filled projection."

During this season, it is important for you to take a look back, see what has worked well for you, and what has not, and make adjustments and changes for future growth. Take your time. Move at your own pace.

However, for each exercise, do not move onto the next until you have committed to *how you will address any areas requiring additional attention or work.*

Write down your commitments and a timeline for addressing or managing them. Remember, what you learn in this season will augment and enhance your growth, healing, and transformation as you move into the next. Your seasonal path eagerly anticipates your investment into it.

1. Reflecting back on all phases of your seasonal process of growth, respond to the following questions.

   ➤ What areas of *SHIFTING* were most challenging to me? Why?

   ➤ In which phases of *SHIFTING* was I most vulnerable? Why?

   ➤ Are there specific conditions or circumstances of *SHIFTING* when I am more likely to struggle? If so, explain in detail.

2. One of the three phases of *SHIFTING Bravely* that tends to be more challenging to most individuals is when A SHIFT Lies Dormant, where we came to understand the role and importance of forms of camouflage.

   Returning to Chapter One, review your forms of camouflage and reflect upon their influence and impact on your process. Then, answer the following questions. Continue to write down how you will commit to addressing or managing them.

   ➤ What *internal* forms of camouflage tend to pull me away from staying true to myself and my growth?

   ➤ What *external* forms of camouflage tend to pull me away from staying true to myself and my growth?

3. Another one of the three phases where we find ourselves being more vulnerable shows up consistently when A SHIFT Takes Root. We learned in Chapter Four how examining and preparing the conditions of our soil as well as assessing its environment is difficult, sensitive work.

   Review your responses to Chapter Four questions and return here for further exploration. Continue to write down how you will commit to addressing or managing them.

   > Are there any additional underlying issues, injuries, or injustices clogging up my soil? If so, identify them.

   > During the critical phase of when A SHIFT Takes Root, did I discover anything else interfering with or stunting my growth as I move forward? If so, explain.

   > What am I still carrying around or spending negative energy on that may be contaminating my soil and restricting future growth? Explain.

   > Did I learn anything about my roots that surprised me or I didn't expect? Explain.

4. The third phase within *SHIFTING Bravely* that often proves to be an ongoing challenge is when A SHIFT Faces Recurring Resistance.

   Review your responses for Chapter Six. Then, return here for further exploration of both internal and external forms of resistance. Continue to write down how you will commit to addressing and managing them.

Internal resistance

> Am I still struggling with self-doubt or shaming life messages? If so, describe what is going on.

> Are there any actions, attitudes, behaviors, thoughts or feelings I tend to deny, minimize, or rationalize that may inhibit future growth? If so, describe them and their impact.

External resistance

> Who or what continues to challenge my growth in ways I find difficult to address? Explain in detail.

> ➢ What boundaries did I implement and then let go of or back down from? Identify and explain why this happened.

> ➢ Where, with whom, and under what circumstances am I most likely not to protect myself and nurture my growth? Why? Explain thoroughly.

> ➢ What relationships do I need to withdraw from or end? Why? Explain how they are impacting you.

> ➢ What environments do I need to withdraw from or move away from? Why? Explain how they are impacting you.

> ➢ What relationships and environments are healthy for my future growth? Identify and explain their influence on you.

5. During Autumn Splendor, it is also critically important to celebrate your successes by identifying what worked well. It is also important to validate yourself in the process.

   Respond to the following questions. As you do so, soak in the beauty and peace of your journey *SHIFTNG* Bravely.

   > ➢ What areas of *SHIFTING* spoke to you and did you connect with more easily? Name them and explain why.

   > ➢ In which phases of *SHIFTING* did you feel your process really take hold and feel your emergence taking form? Name them. Then, explain and describe.

   > ➢ Are there specific lessons, stories, or approaches that inspired, motivated, or encouraged you in your process? If so, explain or describe.

   > ➢ What insights, lessons or messages will you carry with you in your next season of growth? Explain and describe.

   > ➢ Even if a specific practice or principle worked well for you, is there anything you might want to modify or change with the expectation it will augment your future growth? Explain and describe.

6. In A SHIFT Cultivates Future Growth, whose story inspires you the most? Why? What lessons will you take with you as you continue *SHIFTING Bravely*?

Seasonal Closing

"Their [your] healing and growth are an example to
many."

James Blanchard Cisneros

It is 8:50 am. In my home office, I arrange my notepad and adjust the
setting on the side table lamp to a softer glow. Longing for some natural
light but not an overwhelming brightness, I partially close the white
shutters on the east window. Preparing to make my call, I settle into a
comfortable gray rounded chair. A few days ago, I received an email from
a young woman seeking therapy. After a few brief email exchanges, we
agreed on a time for an introduction and a consultation.

While I wait, I think about many of the clients I have been working
with over the past year. A few are at the beginning phases of Winter
Stillness, peeling away their layers of camouflage, listening to their
awakening seeds, and paying attention to their discomfort. Some are in
the depths of movement within Spring Stirrings, doing the necessary hard
work of tending to their roots while others are beginning to experience
their emergence. In the early challenges of Summer Strong, others are
facing and finding their way through all kinds of resistance. A few on this
journey are struggling, falling back into prior patterns of unhealthy
relationships or harmful behaviors. More importantly, they are not giving
up or giving in. They continue choosing to grow, heal, and transform. As
Summer Strong welcomes in Autumn Splendor, several are beginning to
experience the joy and peace of sustaining their "new selves." Being a
part of their journeys, I am both humbled and honored.

My small desk clock draws me back. Its secondhand clicking reminds
me that it is time. I make the call and welcome the voice on the other end.
After a few initial courtesies, I ask her how I can be of help. For the next
thirty minutes, I listen and I reflect. I ask a few questions, probing slightly

into past history with clinical issues and present expectations around therapy. The soft, fragile voice is open but somewhat discouraged. Previous attempts at counseling have not yielded the relief from the discomfort she is experiencing. When I ask what she would hope to gain from counseling this time, she calmly discloses, "I believe there is something deep inside that has not been addressed. I have believed this for a long time...."

For the next few minutes, I talk briefly about my experience within my practice and my methodologies. As I disclose my hope for clients, I also explain the commitment and courage it will take on her part to do the deep hard work. After explaining the paperwork to be filled out and returned, I ask her to take as much time as needed before booking a session. Without hesitation, her voice strengthens a bit as she shares, "I am ready to do the hard work."

After the call, I glance down at the notes on my desk. Another Flower has come my way. Her seed is awakened and it is calling her. She is paying attention to it. She is wanting and willing to tend to its stirrings. Her journey through discomfort begins. Becoming who she is called to be awaits her.

I hear my little clock ticking again. Looking up, I notice how the slanted beams of sunshine cast their rays across the taupe-colored walls of my office. A warmth enters the room and fills my spirit. My mind goes to the courageous individuals from SHIFTING Bravely and their hard work. I am reminded of how their journeys uncovered many of the mysteries behind sustainable change and how their stories are a testament to its legitimacy.

As we bring our time together to a close, let's embrace a hopeful way forward by recalling the transformational truths of the courageous, committed individuals whose stories were shared from "A SHIFT In My Life" and from clients' stories. Because they paid attention to their callings and bravely traveled their pathways, "Their [stories of] healing and growth are an example to many." (Cisneros)

"I am understanding who I really am."

"I am a transformed, emotionally healthier and wiser person."

"Life happened for me, not to me. I am my own woman now."

"I am happy, without working so hard and in sharing my personal story."

"I am able to move away from dis-ease and find inner balance and health."

"I am not what happened to me. I am what I continually choose to become."

"A whole new direction and life opened up for me—a life I never imagined."

"I'm now ten years sober. I have an awesome career helping others find recovery."

"There is a rising up of who I am as a core person. I'm becoming who I am meant to be".

Although our seasonal conversation is closing, the seasonal cycle of emergence never ceases.

Your growth, healing, and transformation await you.

A path lies here—*SHIFTING Bravely.*

Appendix A:
Topics for Deeper Exploration

Purpose

There is much to learn and absorb in each of the chapters of *SHIFTING Bravely*. Throughout the book, there are a myriad of concepts critical in implementing the *SHIFTING* process.

In order to engage more fully with the text, readers are encouraged to utilize the chapter topics and their concepts for deeper exploration. This can either be accomplished within a group or on an individual basis; in a therapeutic setting or within a social gathering such as a book club.

Instructions

After reading each chapter, spend time reflecting on the concepts within it. In a personal journal, make two columns. On one side, write down the chapter, topic, and concept. On the other side, write down your thoughts, feelings, insights, and anything else coming up for you. This is a time to challenge yourself, dig deep, and explore. This is a time to expand personal growth.

In addition to the concepts provided, if you come across other parts of the text that are meaningful or speak to you on a personal level, write those down. Explain their importance

Readers are encouraged to take as much time as needed. This cannot be rushed. Each individual's journey is unique. Each path is traveled as its own pace. And remember, just like the purposeful gardener, the more attention given to the *SHIFTING* process, the more one will derive from it.

Chapter One—A SHIFT Lies Dormant

1. Topic: Forms of camouflage

   ➤ Concept: We are shielded from dormant seeds by various forms of camouflage, disruptions and diversions consuming our lives and often controlling their course.

2. Topic: Borderline Personality Disorder

   ➤ Concept: These reactive, unstable, and impulsive behaviors are an attempt to "make frantic efforts to avoid real or imagined abandonment" (DSM-5, p. 663). In other words, fearing they [individuals who suffer with BPD] are being rejected or abandoned, they will turn on others suddenly or reject them first to avoid such feelings.

3. Topic: Camouflage is in anyone or anything pulling our attention outward

   ➤ Concept: It [camouflage] is any source of external influence or interest in which we choose to invest ourselves. And it is when we begin to over-invest into someone or something—where our worth is determined predominantly by our degree of investment—that we unwittingly place ourselves in a posture of unknowing.

Chapter Two—A SHIFT Is Awakened

1. Topic: Seeds await their calling

   ➤ Concept: The calling, signaling us how our current ways of being are no longer serving our wellbeing, emanates from a single source. That source is discomfort.

2. Topic: Conditions necessary for a call to be heard

   ➤ Concept: The conditions are threefold. However, depending on the unique circumstances of each person's experience, their order of presentation may vary.

      • One condition is the following: we realize and accept we no longer are able to manage our discomfort.

      • A second condition is as important: we have come to realize and accept the discomfort is managing us.

- The third condition essential to the awakening process, in which a call is heard, is the presence of a trigger or triggers.

  ➢ Concept: When a trigger/s is blended together with an acceptance of both our lack of control over our discomfort and its management of us, A SHIFT Is Awakened.

  ➢ Concept: Each and every time we wish we were doing something else, or any time we envy another person's life, or whenever we make excuses or get angry at ourselves for our current state of being—we need to stop. We need to recognize these thoughts are messengers. They are calling us to awaken.

  ➢ Concept: Each and every time we dismiss or ignore them [messengers or triggers], we sabotage another opportunity for an awakening and for growth. With each missed calling, we exile our seeds back into dormancy.

3. Topic: A form of camouflage—codependency

  ➢ Concept: For our purposes, we will define codependency as an over-investment into someone, all in an attempt to rescue, control, or change a person and his behaviors.

Chapter Three—A SHIFT Awaiting Attention

1. Topic: How we position ourselves to hear a calling

  ➢ Concept: In the critical moments of our seeds awakening, we are being summoned to assume an alternate mindset and posture. In this final phase of Winter Stillness, we are being called to position ourselves inwardly for A SHIFT Awaiting Attention.

  ➢ Concept: This time, at that critical moment of awakening, Jazmine paused and turned inward. Like a gardener taking time for observation, assessment, and re-examination, she quieted her mind and recalled honorable memories from generations past and their ensuing legacies. Her seeds once again lie awakened, eagerly Awaiting Attention.

Chapter Four—A SHIFT Takes Root

1. Topic: Certain conditions must be met for seeds to grow.

   ➤ Concept: These toxic particles (in our soil) are like blocks of hardened clay, acting as barriers against the process of germination where roots reach into the earth while stems begin to stretch upwards. The beginnings of growth will be stunted or sabotaged if the roots cannot move through porous soil in order to access water for nourishment.

   ➤ Concept: Gardeners spend a great deal of time examining and preparing their soil. Even after seeds have been planted, gardeners remain mindful of the soil's constitution and condition.

   ➤ Concept: Not only is it necessary to have a healthy balanced composition of soil, but the growth environment must meet certain requirements as well.

Chapter Five—A SHIFT Emerges

1. Topic: Tending to our soil and its environment

   ➤ Concept: At any time during the process of *SHIFTING Bravely*, the conditions of our soil can and will change. And, this is true for our environments as well. We must return to the process of examining, preparing, and assessing our soil and its surroundings.

2. Topic: SHIFTS emerged largely, but not entirely, from two distinct paths

   ➤ Concept: Example of a cognitive-based emerging SHIFT:

     • A time of reflection (or other cognitive processes) begins the process of SHIFTING our beliefs, feelings, thoughts, and attitudes.

     • These SHIFTS in our beliefs, feelings, thoughts, and attitudes lead to action steps.

     • This, in turn, stimulates more reflection (or other cognitive processes)

- ➢ Concept: Example of an action-based emerging SHIFT:
  - Actionable steps begin the process of SHIFTING
  - As a result of these actions, SHIFTS begins to emerge in our beliefs, feelings, thoughts, and attitudes.
  - These dynamic beliefs, feelings, thoughts, and attitudes become stimuli for further action.

3. Topic: Considerations in action-based paths
   - ➢ Concept: Sometimes, we are required to take action steps even when we are uncertain as to their potential benefit to our growing process.
   - ➢ Concept: Even when we want to change our direction, it can be very scary. There is nothing comfortable about uncertainty or risk.

4. Topic: Relationship between action-based and cognitive-based paths of emergence
   - ➢ Concept: Whether the emergence is cognitive-based or action-based, we see how closely interrelated they are. Our beliefs, feelings, thoughts, and attitudes about ourselves largely determine our actions and behaviors. And the reverse is true.

5. Topic: Critical reminders for entering a path of emergence
   - ➢ Concept: First, when A SHIFT Takes Root, rather than focusing on things outside of ourselves or placing needs of others above our own, we are called upon to be brave, to turn inward, and tend to our soil.
   - ➢ Concept: Second, when A SHIFT Emerges, we are also called to make a critical decision—to choose our "self." No matter how big or small the action step is before us or how significant or insignificant the cognitive challenge may be, we must choose our "self."
   - ➢ Concept: Regardless of how the calling shows up, the pathways into self-growth are endless. They are ours for the choosing.

6. Topic: Third important path of emergence

> ➤ Concept: This path takes place within a therapeutic setting—between client and professional therapist—and it is based on trust, connection, and unconditional positive regard. It is within the safety of the therapeutic relationship and within the shared space of comfort and mutual respect where little SHIFTS show up, connect with other related little SHIFTS, linking together to form larger SHIFTS that in turn deepen roots and clear the way for a rising stem.

Chapter Six—A SHIFT Faces Recurring Resistance

1. Topic: Recurring resistance is present throughout all phases of SHIFTING

> ➤ Concept: Thus far, throughout a seasonal process of self-growth, we have witnessed within stories from "A SHIFT In My Life," as well as through clients' stories, countless occurrences where individuals encountered internal and external forms of resistance, embraced them, and moved through them.

2. Topic: Internal resistance

> ➤ Concept: We are coming to understand how different forms of internal resistance are a natural occurrence within our unique journeys. We must not be ashamed or embarrassed by their presence or intrusion into our process. We must acknowledge them and address them, one at a time, as our transformation continues to form and flourish.

> ➤ Concept: Whether we are experiencing a strong and sizable emergence or a more subtle and steady one, there is often an eerily quiet and extremely confusing form of internal resistance taking residence within our being—a state of unease.

> ➤ Concept: This vulnerability is normal. Whether we are entering into a new career, embracing a new phase of recovering, engaging in new relationships, or embarking on new adventures, discoveries, or opportunities, there will be a mixture of accomplishment and trepidation. In our new vulnerability, one minute we will doubt ourselves and

everything we are doing. The next moment, we will know we are precisely where we are supposed to be.

3. Topic: External resistance

> Concept: When we come up against formidable external forces of resistance embedded within social, cultural, organizational, institutional norms or in any system where there is a power differential with potential severe consequences at stake, we each must decide what is best for us, our integrity, and our process of self-growth.

> Concept: As we have learned, external forms of resistance show up in social norms, regulations, rules, and laws often posing a significant challenge to our emerging process. At the same time, one of most difficult faces of recurring external resistance shows up in our lives on a more personal level— our relationships with family and friends.

4. Topic: Tolerance levels and resistance

> Concept: This is a sign of increased awareness into our process and what is needed to maintain its integrity. And like a gardener who carefully monitors the impact of environmental elements on growth and makes calculated adjustments, we too must assess what nourishes us and what does not.

Chapter Seven—A SHIFT Is Sustained

1. Topic: The organic nature of sustainability

> Concept: But Summer Strong was not willing to succumb to such a fate. To her astonishment, the garden inhabitants not only survived, they thrived. Without a drip system in place, there was simply no explanation, except one. Tethered to their organic strength nurtured and fostered deeply within, the resilient bodies of growth sustained themselves. The bountiful array of vegetables huddled beneath the leafy canopies was a testament to it.

> Concept: Moving into the fullness of Summer Strong, we too can claim that strength. One of the beautiful gifts of *SHIFTING Bravely* is *knowing* how our growth is capable of sustaining us. Our *knowing* is evidenced by a clear

differentiation between our truths about ourselves and our ways of being prior to our SHIFT in comparison to during and after our SHIFT. These news truths show up in our attitudes, beliefs, and feelings as well as in our actions, behaviors, and choices.

2. Topic: First organic representation of when A SHIFT Is Sustained

    "As you are shifting, you will begin to realize you are not the same person you used to be."

    ➤ Concept: I believe, of the five areas of organic representation, "Beginning to realize we are not the same person we used to be" is one of the most remarkable and meaningful internal rewards of our journey. It is important to note how it may start to show up in little shifts earlier in our seasonal process of self-growth, and this realization can serve as an incredible catalyst as we move through each seasonal phase. However, it is usually much more pronounced after our SHIFT has emerged more fully and has become more thoroughly integrated within our being.

    ➤ Concept: It is the deliberate acknowledgement of this new truth—*we are not the same person we used to be*—that sustains us to our new ways of being and strengthens us as we continue to grow.

3. Second organic representation of when A SHIFT Is Sustained

    "The things you used to tolerate have become intolerable."

    ➤ Concept: Boundary work is hard and it is necessary for our protection. Boundaries create space for truth to thrive.

    ➤ Concept: We must be brutally honest about how our expectations of any relationship might impact us and we must be intentional about our degree of investment.

4. Third organic representation of when A SHIFT Is Sustained

    "When you once remained quiet, you are now speaking your truth."

    ➤ Concept: Even after our SHIFT has emerged, there is no guarantee we will not be further shamed, blamed, or judged for speaking our truths. There is always some degree of risk in sharing them.

➢ Concept: I believe you will *know* when you are ready to speak your truths.

➢ Concept: Speaking our truths is not about how others will receive them. Speaking our truths is about us—validating our growth's sustainability by affirming we are rooted in our truths.

5. Fourth organic representation of when A SHIFT Is Sustained

"Where you once battled and argued, you are now choosing to remain silent."

➢ Concept: I believe when we are truly grounded in our growth and its strength, we are at peace with ourselves and with others. Battles or arguments we had within ourselves and with others in proving our truths or substantiating our growth are no longer important. They are no longer necessary. In our peace, we are choosing to silence past representations such as anger, resentment, and blame. Because of our growth, we are choosing to honor it in healthy ways. In doing so, we find ourselves once again taking on the posture of a gardener—being still, listening, staying open, and giving ourselves time for further internal strengthening.

➢ Concept: When we are in the beginning phases of our seasonal process, it is common and understandable to be angry, argumentative, and reactionary, especially to those who have contributed to our wounding. However, as more time passes and *we begin to realize we are not the same person we used to be,* we also begin reframing our perceptions to reflect our current truths. This does not minimize the harm others have caused. However, this hurt no longer holds us hostage to them.

➢ Concept: When we remain open to new discoveries and insights regarding our experiences, our defensive posture takes a back seat to welcoming in an understanding of them. It is with deeper insight we find ourselves *remaining silent within,* settling into our peace and calm.

    ➤ Concept: When A SHIFT Is Sustained, we are anchored in our truths. And when the waters around us are unpredictable or choppy, our *knowing* of our truths secures us. We do not react to our unsafe environments or adversaries. *Where we once battled and argued, we are now choosing to remain silent.* We now choose a peaceful response.

6.   Fifth organic representation of when A SHIFT Is Sustained

    "You are beginning to understand the value of your voice and there are some situations that no longer deserve your time, energy, and focus."

    ➤ Concept: The degree we love ourselves, take care of ourselves, and respect ourselves is a predictor to the degree others will do the same. In other words, how well we treat ourselves will teach others how to treat us. Others will not love us unconditionally if we do not love ourselves first.

    ➤ Concept: The more secure we are in ourselves and our truths, the more discerning we become. First, in our discernment we are clear about who to trust and who not to. Second, like a gardener whose deep *knowing* fosters precision in decision-making, our internalized *knowing* focuses our thinking and behaviors.

    ➤ Concept: The posture of discernment comes with time, experience, patience, and resilience. It cannot be rushed. However, it *will* show itself. We *will* feel it. We *will* act on it. The more internalized our truths become, the more we will be able to discern who or what is deserving of our voice, time, energy, and focus.

    ➤ Concept: In our understanding and application of it, empowerment means *valuing our voice* by *voicing our value.* In other words, self-empowerment is a clear, confident, authentic representation of our truths and our growth. When we are *valuing our voice,* we do not seek to dominate or demand. And when we are *voicing our value,* we do so by representing our strong belief in who we are as we thoughtfully and respectfully take control of our lives.

    ➤ Concept: It is when our SHIFT solidifies within us, that we find ourselves unable, unwilling, and incapable of compromising our truths or our ways of being. It is simply non-negotiable as we are *rooted in our truths*. In the Flower's words, "I'm becoming who I am meant to be."

Chapter Eight—A SHIFT Cultivates Future Growth

1. Topic: The purposes of Autumn Splendor

   ➤ Concept: During Autumn Splendor, we must take time to reflect upon self-growth and closely take stock of all phases of our process. First, this is a time for us to look back, glean from what we have learned, and make adjustments or changes for the ensuing season. Second, it is also a time to celebrate our successes, identify what worked well, and plan for future growth.

2. Topic: Self-examination of A SHIFT Lies Dormant

   ➤ Concept: During this period of self-examination, I ask clients to recall their forms of camouflage, to name them, and to conduct periodic inventories on the degree of their presence or interference in their lives. By conducting this intentional practice, we position ourselves more intuitively—paying attention to an awakening of seeds during our next season of growth.

   ➤ Concept: Although numerous forms of camouflage were discussed in Chapter One, the presence of shaming life messages is perhaps the most destructive force moving against future growth.

3. Topic: Self-examination of A SHIFT Takes Root

   ➤ Concept: In reviewing our seasonal process of growth, it is critical we take a brutally honest inventory of our soil's condition, what areas were not as strong or healthy, and where there may need to be minor adjustments or major changes.

   ➤ Concept: During Autumn Splendor, there is no shame in identifying or rediscovering areas of needed attention. There is only disappointment if we are not observant and open to these vulnerable areas. Looking forward to the next season, we view increasing our awareness and knowledge of our soil's richness as powerful companions for expanding our growth.

4. Topic: A SHIFT Faces Recurring Resistance

    ➤ Concept: Like the wise gardener who is proactively taking measures to secure the soil's dampness, we must do all we can to safeguard our "new self." There will always be forces continuing to test and challenge us. Some of them will be out of our control. The beauty is we will learn from them and plan accordingly.

    ➤ Concept: In planning for the next season, our degree of future growth is dependent upon the degree of maintaining our soil's healthy structure, its levels of nutrients, and the ongoing implementation of protective boundaries. In my own recovery, in my years of working with clients, and in the stories from "A SHIFT In My Life," I believe that boundary work is one of the hardest skills to integrate into our lives on a consistent basis. And yet, just like crop rotation, it creates the healthy space for expanding present emergence and for cultivating future growth.

5. Topic: Celebrating our successes and affirming ourselves

    ➤ Concept: We have come to understand that it is important to look back and discover what we want to do differently in order to *cultivate future growth*. However, it is just as important to celebrate our journey of *SHIFTING Bravely*. It is important to call out our successes and to identify what worked well. It is also critical to affirm ourselves in the process.

    ➤ Concept: We are more likely to advance our growth if we know in advance what contributes to it. This is not only a time to celebrate our hard work, but it is critical to acknowledge what works for each of us.

    ➤ Concept: *Knowing* what is working for us is critical. *Acknowledging* and *affirming* its benefits condition our soil for future growth.

    ➤ Concept: As we move through our growing process, we must be patient with ourselves, emerge at our own pace, and always remain open to growth messages coming our way.

Early in our process we may not connect with tools, strategies, or lessons. In our time of reflection and self-examination, it is important to return to or revisit prior resources and avenues for support, especially if there is a nudging within us.

Appendix B: Letter of Invitation

MFT 39156
INVITATION TO PARTICIPATE IN AN INDEPENDENT PROJECT:
A SHIFT In My Life

Invitation to Participate

I, Holli Kenley, invite you to participate in an independent study—A SHIFT In My Life—conducted by Holli Kenley. Participation will consist of responding to a written questionnaire (5 questions). Your participation in this project is voluntary. Please read the information below and ask questions about anything you do not understand before deciding whether or not to participate. Contact holli@hollikenley.com.

Background on Study

Although I can recall many shifts in my life, two years ago I experienced a powerful shift after which I developed a deeper insight into its significance within the process of growth. In addition, my interest in *shifting* intensified after returning to my private practice as a Licensed Marriage & Family Therapist. Over the past two years, I have had the opportunity to assist clients with their own shifts and to witness their personal transformations and growth. Thus, I am eager to learn more from your stories.

Purpose of Study

1) The purpose of studying "A SHIFT In My Life" is to explore the conditions, processes, and variables that contributed to a transformative experience in your life.

2) For the purpose of this study, a shift is defined as the following:

   an unexpected or unpredictable compelling transformation in your beliefs, perceptions, ways of thinking, or truths about you, someone else, or something.

3) For the purpose of this study, you are free to share any shift in your life, whether minor or major. However, this shift must have led to outcomes that altered your life in constructive, healing, or empowering ways.

Required Consent to Participate and Instructions for Participation

If you are interested in participating, please contact me at holli@hollikenley.com.

I will provide you with the required Informed Consent to Participate and the Instructions for Participation.

Thank you.

Holli Kenley, MA, LMFT

Acknowledgements

From its genesis to its publication, *SHIFTING Bravely* is the combined hard work and commitment of extraordinary individuals.

Inspiration: Thank you to my daughter, Alexis. Your mentoring of me regarding the gardening process and modeling of a purposeful gardener served as a metaphorical inspiration for creating a process of self-growth. The standard of excellence you approach any endeavor is remarkable.

Seeds: Thank you to the participants from "A SHIFT In My Life," along with anonymous clients. Your courageous stories of self-growth provided rich, authentic content to illustrate the process of shifting. Thank you to the Flower. I will carry your story with me, always.

Skillful Caretakers: Thank you to my editors—Dan Kenley, Lani Stoner, and Dr. Bob Rich.

Thank you to my husband, Dan. Your ability to edit my manuscript by listening to each and every word is a gift beyond explanation. Your acute sense of choosing just the right words elevates comprehension and enhances coherence. You make my work more reader-friendly.

Thank you to my friend, fellow therapist, and diligent gardener of my manuscript, Lani Stoner. Your skills in editing, revising, and refining are the talents every writer dreams of and depends on. Your profound insight and professional integrity with which you approach your work is evident in every aspect of the editing process. You make me a better writer.

Thank you to Dr. Bob Rich. The universe, connecting us later in the process of writing *SHIFTING Bravely*, knew exactly when to bring your editing expertise, professional experience, personal standard of excellence, and empathic lens to this work. You are a gift.

Harvester: Thank you, Loving Healing Press, Inc. and publisher Victor Volkman. Your openness and willingness to embrace my work, as it shifts and changes, speaks to our long and lasting collaborative relationship.

You and your support make my passion come to life—bringing growth, healing, and transformation to others.

About the Author

Holli Kenley is a California Licensed Marriage and Family Therapist and a California State Licensed Teacher. She holds a Master's Degree in Psychology with an emphasis in Marriage, Family, and Child Counseling. She has worked in a variety of settings: a women's shelter, a counseling center, and in private practice. Counseling with teens, adults, and couples, Holli's areas of specialized training and experience include sexual abuse and trauma, betrayal, codependency, cyber bullying, relapse, screen dependence, proactive parenting, and the process of growth, healing, and transformation. Prior to and during her career as a therapist, Holli taught for thirty years in public education.

In addition to maintaining a private practice, Holli Kenley, MA, MFT, also works in the field of psychology as an author, speaker, and workshop presenter. Holli is the author of ten recovery / self-empowerment books. She has been a six-time peer presenter at the California Association of Marriage and Family Therapists' Annual State Conferences and a featured or keynote speaker at college level clinical programs, state and national advocacy organizations, and educational institutions. Holli has been a guest on over 100 podcasts as well as on TV speaking on issues of wellness.

Holli lives with her husband, Dan, in Southern California.

For more information about Holli or to contact her for your next conference, workshop, or speaking opportunity, please visit www.hollikenley.com.

Bibliography

Beattie, M. (2011). *Codependent no more. How to stop controlling others and start caring for yourself.* Center City, MIN: Hazelden.

Brown, B. (2017). *Braving the wilderness: The quest for true belonging and the courage to stand alone.* New York, NY: Random House.

Brown, B. (2012*). Daring greatly: How the courage to be vulnerable transforms the way we live, love, parent, and lead.* New York, NY: Penguin Random House.

Brown, B. (2017). *Rising Strong: How the ability to reset transforms the way we live, love, parent, and lead.* New York, NY: Random House.

Brown, B. (2020). *The gifts of imperfection: 10th anniversary edition.* New York, NY: Random House.

Diagnostic and statistical manual of mental disorders: DSM-5 (5th ed.). (2017). Arlington, VA: American Psychiatric Association.

Doyle, G. (2020). *Untamed.* New York, NY: The Dial Press.

Dyer, W. W. (2009). *The shift: Taking your life from ambition to meaning.* Carlsbad, CA: Hay House.

Gold, G. D. (2018*). I will be complete: A memoir.* Sceptre. Great Britain.

Golomb, G. (1995). *Trapped in the mirror: Adult children of narcissists in the struggle for self.* New York, NY: William Murrow.

Kenley, H. (2016). *Breaking through betrayal: And recovering the peace within* (2nd ed.). Ann Arbor, MI: Loving Healing Press.

Kenley, H. (2018). *Daughters betrayed by their mothers: Moving from brokenness to wholeness* . Ann Arbor, MI: Loving Healing Press.

Kenley, H. (2020). *Mountain air: Relapsing and finding the way back one breath at a time.* Ann Arbor, MI: Loving Healing Press.

Lees, A. B. (2019, April 18). Posttraumatic Growth. Retrieved October 12, 2020, from https://www.psychologytoday.com/us/blog/surviving-thriving/201904/posttraumatic-growth

Marvel, R. (2020). *Healing childhood trauma: Transforming pain into purpose with post-traumatic growth.* Ann Arbor, MI: Loving Healing Press.

McGowen, R. (2018). *Brave.* Great Britain: HQ, an imprint of Harper Collins Publishers, LTD.

Paler, J. (2020, October 14). Shadow Work: Seven Steps To Heal The Wounded Self. Retrieved January 3, 2021, from https://hackspirit.com/7-shadow-work-techniques-to-heal-the-wounded- self/

Perry, B. D., & Winfrey, O. (2021). *What happened to you?: Conversations on trauma, resilience, and healing.* New York: Flatiron Books.

Robbins, M. (2017). *The five second rule: Transform your life, work, and confidence with everyday courage.* United States: A Savio Republic Book.

Singer, M. (2007). *The untethered soul: The journey beyond.* Oakland, CA: New Harbinger Publications.

Tedeschi, R. G. (2020, June 16). Growth After Trauma. Retrieved October 12, 2020, from https://hbr.org/2020/07/growth-after-trauma

Westover, T. (2019). *Educated: A memoir.* New York, NY: Random House (Large Print).

Index

W

Electronic Media Can Endanger
As Well As Empower Your Kids

In this decade, our digital world has grown exponentially as has the degree of time both adults and children are spending on their screens. Not surprisingly, researchers are discovering a myriad of unhealthy behaviors associated with excessive screen time. In *Power Down & Parent Up*, Kenley expands on her groundbreaking book *Cyber Bullying No More*, giving parents/guardians effective strategies to integrate into their lives and their children's. How can we navigate a tech-driven world and raise tech-healthy children?

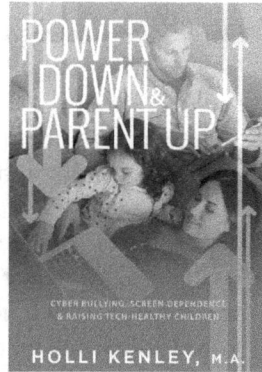

- Tackle cyber bullying head-on by implementing a concise "Parent Up" approach with proven strategies for *Protection, Intervention, and Prevention.*

- "Power Down" on screen dependence and become fully informed about its growing health concerns and consequences.

- Learn *Seven Proactive Practices* such as goal setting and creating a family plan to reduce screen time.

- Discover *Four Healthy Guidelines* to add to our parenting toolbox such as learning how to communicate about the false nature of cyber worth and cultivate our children's real worth.

"Rather imply that families can return to some idealistic less complicated time without Facebook, sexting, social networks, and Twitter, and whatever else comes along, Kenley's booklet will help parents mitigate possible harm to their children as they integrate this technology hopefully into healthy lives and relationships."

--Ronald Mah, M.A. LMFT, author of *Difficult Behavior in Early Childhood* and *The One Minute Temper Tantrum Solution*

"Holli addresses children's readiness for technology as well as rules, contracts and education for parents to consider for their children as they introduce or allow entry of new technology into their lives."

--Lani Stoner, Marriage and Family Therapist

paperback * hardcover * eBook * audiobook

Learn more at www.HolliKenley.com

The daughters' stories touch upon the deepest and darkest of pains: knowing you have a mother... but you don't.

Daughters Betrayed By Their Mothers: Moving From Brokenness To Wholeness is an intimate exploration into the lives of daughters who were wounded by their mothers and who chose wellness over victimhood. Each daughter's unique story of recovery is a testament to the power of choice, perseverance and resilience. Readers are invited to journey alongside the daughters, grabbing hold of healing lifelines and moving from broken places to whole spaces within.

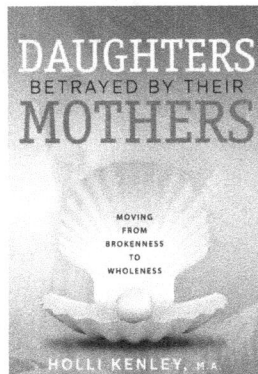

- Do you feel your mother did not "show up" for you in the ways you needed?

- Because of your mother's role in your life, do you feel like you were "not enough?"

- Do you wonder if it is possible to heal from the brokenness that comes from being wounded by your mother?

If you answered "yes" to any of these questions, the "Daughters" warmly welcome you.

"There are tears of both sorrow and joy in the beautiful, brave stories of harm and hope. Daughters Betrayed By Their Mothers changed my life."
      --Charlotte Carson, Editorial Director, ClearLifeMagazine.com

"*Daughters Betrayed By Their Mothers* is heartrending and uplifting; dark and optimistic; painful and inspirational. A profound human document."
      --Sam Vaknin, author of *Malignant Self-Love: Narcissism Revisited*

"Powerful, reflective, and reassuring to all who read it, Holli Kenley's *Daughters Betrayed By Their Mothers* reminds us that no matter what hurt we have experienced, the opportunity to heal and be whole is always possible."
      --Cyrus Webb, media personality, author, and speaker

paperback * hardcover * eBook * audiobook

Learn more at www.HolliKenley.com

Your Personalized Work-out Regime for Adjusting Your Approach to *Parent-Child Relationships*

PILATES *for* PARENTING

STRETCH YOURSELF and STRENGTHEN YOUR FAMILY

HOLLI KENLEY, M.A.

When it comes to implementing healthy roles and tackling heavy responsibilities of being a parent, Pilates For Parenting targets five strategic areas. The goals of the Warm Up, 3 Workouts and Cool Down include:

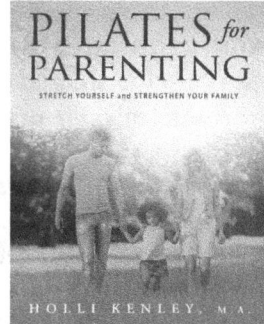

- Increasing awareness regarding the importance of parenting

- Strengthening the skill of being present for your children

- Fortifying the skill of doing what is best for your children

- Honing the skill of meeting your children's needs

- Increasing accountability as you become purposeful in your parenting

"This is not your normal 'how to' parenting book. *Pilates For Parenting* helps us, as caregivers, get to the heart of parenting, take time to evaluate what to do and become more in tune with our children. I will be using the parenting workouts myself and with my clients."
--Jill Osborne, EDS, LPC, CPCS, RTS, Author, *Same Feels Better Now!*

"In the digital age in which we live, we are often too distracted by our smartphones, social media sites and television screens. *Pilates For Parenting* just might be the best method for reconnecting with your children and developing stronger relationships."
--Thomas Kersting, MA, LPC, Author, *Disconnected: How To Reconnect Our Digitally Distracted Kids*

"The text, workouts, activities and guiding exercises in *Pilates For Parenting* will equip readers with their own personalized, practical, effective game-plan as they navigate the ups and downs of becoming nurturing, protective and wise parents."
--Judy Herzanek, Changing Lives Foundation, Co-author, *Why Don't They Just Quit? Hope for families struggling with addiction*

paperback * hardcover * eBook

Learn more at www.HolliKenley.com

Deep down inside, each of us knows what our truths are.
It is forgivable to lose them...
it is unforgivable not to reclaim them...

Mountain Air: Relapsing And Finding The Way Back One Breath At A Time is a brutally honest personal narrative detailing a painful decent into relapse and a powerful journey back to recovering.
Without condemnation but with passion and purpose, Mountain Air ...

- Embraces individuals who have abandoned their authentic ways of being for a life of personal neglect, indulgence, or self-destruction.

- Speaks to individuals who have betrayed their healing tenets - the addict who has lost his sobriety, the abused who has returned to her abuser, or the codependent who continues to rescue the uncontrollable.

- Reaches out to individuals who have maintained a life of stability and wellness, but who are eroding over time – and losing their sense of self and of spirit.

Mountain Air is for any individual who has experienced relapse and who is fighting to find his way back...

- By inviting readers to take a journey with the author as she shares time-tested lessons in the recovering process.

- By providing thoughtful and accountable exercises with each chapter that guide the reader in the reclaiming and sustaining of their truths.

paperback * hardcover * eBook

Learn more at **www.HolliKenley.com**

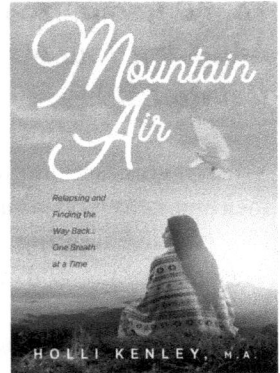

www.ingramcontent.com/pod-product-compliance
Lightning Source LLC
Chambersburg PA
CBHW072239270326
41930CB00010B/2199